Reading the Bible and the Confessions

The Presbyterian Way

JACK ROGERS

Geneva Press
Louisville, Kentucky

Book design by Sharon Adams
Cover design by Jennifer K. Cox

First edition

Published by Geneva Press
Louisville, Kentucky

This book is printed on acid-free paper that meets the American National Standards Institute Z39.48 standard. ⊗

PRINTED IN THE UNITED STATES OF AMERICA

99 00 01 02 03 04 05 06 07 08 — 10 9 8 7 6 5 4 3 2

Library of Congress Cataloging-in-Publication Data

Rogers, Jack Bartlett.
    Reading the Bible and the Confessions : the Presbyterian way / Jack Rogers.
        p.   cm.
    Includes bibliographical references.
    ISBN 0-664-50046-3 (alk. paper)
    1. Presbyterian Church (U.S.A.)—Doctrines.   Bible—
Hermeneutics.   3. Presbyterian Church (U.S.A.)   Book of
confessions.   4. Presbyterian Church (U.S.A.)—Creeds.   I. Title.
BX8969.5.R64   1999
230'.51—dc21   99-24404
                                                                      CIP

To my wife, Sharon Rogers,
Who can see the infinite potential in every child,

And whose work with and writing about severely speech-impaired children has profound theological meaning.

Other books by Jack Rogers

Claiming the Center:
Churches and Conflicting Worldviews

Presbyterian Creeds:
A Guide to the Book of Confessions

CONTENTS

PREFACE

When I began a long-overdue sabbatical leave in January of 1998, I had no intention of writing a book. I needed time away from administrative duties to read and think. Due to the urging of my friend and dean, Ron White, I had a place, a most marvelous place to work—the Huntington Library in San Marino, California. The Huntington, one of the premier research libraries in the United States, specializes in seventeenth- through early twentieth-century British and American history and literature. I am grateful to the Readers Services staff and other Readers at the Huntington for receiving me and providing both a carrel and an unparalleled environment for scholarly concentration.

I also had a concern. At a conference in the fall of 1997, I had discovered what I should have long known—that in the 1950s, the Presbyterian churches, North and South, had amended the Westminster Confession of Faith to make it possible for divorced and remarried people to serve as office bearers. Amending the Westminster Confession in the 1950s was a very big step. I began to ponder the process by which the church changes its mind about the interpretation of Scripture and the Confessions.

And I had two invitations. I have taught and written on the history of biblical and confessional interpretation more times than I can remember. I had agreed to just two long-standing invitations to lecture during my eight-and-a-half-month sabbatical. The first was to give eight lectures on interpreting the Confessions to the Association of Stated Clerks in Montreat, just before the Charlotte General Assembly in June of 1998. The other was to give six lectures to a group of midwestern Presbyterian pastors at the Omaha Seminary Foundation School for Pastors at Hastings College.

After I finished the two sets of lectures, I realized that I had a small book in the making. I had brought six months of new research on how the church had changed its mind on slavery and segregation, the role of women, and divorce and remarriage to my previous background in the history of biblical and confessional interpretation.

I am grateful to Stephanie Egnotovich, Executive Editor of Westminster John Knox Press, for encouraging me to try to shape this material into a book for the church. I am thankful to Tom Long, the Director of Geneva Press, for seeing the possibility of using this book as an educational resource for the denomination. Special thanks go to Stephanie for editing the manuscript and red-marking every page in her determination that this material would be presented in a form accessible to a broad readership. If it achieves that goal, the credit is hers.

Several good friends took time from their very compacted schedules to read the manuscript. I am grateful to my San Francisco Theological Seminary colleagues, Ron White, Elizabeth Nordquist, Cyris Moon, and Bob Coote. Friends and colleagues at a distance, Louis Weeks and Barbara Wheeler, also made valuable comments. I have learned from all of them, but of course take full and final responsibility for the ways in which I have responded.

My thanks to Clifton Kirkpatrick for making available the small but excellent library in the Office of the General Assembly. Joe Small and his staff in the Office of Theology and Worship were generous in identifying and sending me copies of denominational reports and Minutes of the General Assembly.

Finally, as always, I am thankful for the love and support of my wife, Sharon, who although deeply engrossed in finishing her own Ph.D. dissertation has always had time to encourage me in my writing.

Jack Rogers

Advent 1998

INTRODUCTION

Interpreting Scripture
and the Confessions

Presbyterians are not do-it-your-selfers. We make decisions as a community. Those decisions are based on our traditional sources of authority and guidance and the continuing work of the Holy Spirit in the life of the church. Our guides to belief and practice are Scripture and the heritage of reflection on Scripture found in the *Book of Confessions*. All officeholders in the Presbyterian church—deacons, elders, and ministers of Word and Sacrament—must answer "Yes" to this question: "Will you fulfill your office in obedience to Jesus Christ, under the authority of Scripture, and be continually guided by our confessions?"[1]

That question is easy to answer affirmatively but hard to implement in practice. Surely most office bearers answer it with sincerity. Sources of authority are helpful, however, only if they are understood. The practical questions, then, become: What do Scripture and the Confessions say? and, How do we interpret their meaning for us?

Answering those questions is not a simple task. We are talking about a Bible with sixty-six books written over a period from at least 1000 B.C. until into the second century A.D. Their ancient Near Eastern historical and cultural contexts are unfamiliar to most of us.

The Presbyterian *Book of Confessions* consists of eleven documents written from the fourth century A.D. to the late twentieth century. They point us to Christ and to the great themes of the Christian faith. The Confessions are guides to how our forebears in the faith interpreted the Bible. However, they also exhibit the characteristics of many different cultures and customs, some of them quite foreign to our own way of understanding and interpreting Scripture. So, it seems that the Confessions, which interpret Scripture, must themselves be interpreted.

Presbyterians have thought about these issues. Representative committees composed of academic experts and ordinary folk have studied them. General Assemblies have approved guidelines for interpreting Scripture and using the Confessions. Most Presbyterians, however, seem unaware of these efforts. We tend to struggle with each new issue as if we were the first to confront it. That need not be so.

American Presbyterians began to struggle with significant issues even before the founding of the nation and the Presbyterian denomination itself. We have a rich history of interpreting Scripture and the Confessions. Using the resources of both the Huntington Library and the Office of the General Assembly, I have traced how American Presbyterians dealt with three great personal and societal issues: slavery and segregation; the role of women; and divorce and remarriage. In each case, over time, the church dramatically changed its understanding of the teaching of Scripture. In each case, in response to changing social situations, the Confessions were amended or a new confessional statement was developed.

This history of how we Presbyterians have actually interpreted Scripture and the Confessions can be instructive. If we can understand the pattern of our historical practice, we can learn better how to handle similar personal and societal problems in the future.

THE STRUCTURE OF THIS BOOK

In this book I explain the policies and the practices of the church. I provide commentary on our confessional and governmental heritage, and I offer suggestions for practical application of our constitutional documents informed by our history. I hope to stimulate the individual and communal use of Scripture and the Confessions so that our methods of interpretation will be in accord with our Presbyterian policies and practices. We can learn from the past so that we do not make the same kinds of mistakes over and over again.

This book is in two parts. Part 1 deals with interpreting an authoritative Scripture. Part 2 deals with interpreting the Confessions in our *Book of Confessions*. The two parts have a parallel structure. In each part I begin with general discussion about the kind of interpretation that is appropriate to the subject: Scripture or the Confessions. Then I note the official policy of the Presbyterian church regarding, first, the interpretation of Scripture, and, second, the interpretation of the Confessions. Then, in each part I identify and discuss seven guidelines for interpretation.

The guidelines for interpreting Scripture, covered in Part 1, were adopted by the United Presbyterian Church in the United States of America in 1982. They were supported and elaborated in guidelines adopted by the Presbyterian Church in the United States in 1983. These predecessor denominations of our present church, the Presbyterian Church (U.S.A.), bequeathed to us a common approach to interpreting Scripture that will benefit us.

In Part 2 I develop seven guidelines for interpreting the *Book of Confessions* that closely parallel the guidelines for interpreting Scripture. Although certain General Assemblies have reflected on the issue of confessional interpretation, it has not been dealt with in as direct a manner as has the interpretation of Scripture. Similarly, theologians and historians of doctrine have written about the content of the Confessions in our *Book of Confessions*. Nothing, however, has been written that deals directly with how the Confessions are appropriately interpreted.

I use a generally parallel pattern in developing each set of seven guidelines. In each of the seven guidelines for interpreting Scripture, I begin with an explanation of the guideline; then I indicate its confirmation in the Confessions, and finally I point to some practical consequences. In each of the seven guidelines for interpreting the Confessions I provide an extended illustration of the church's historical practice, indicate what the church's present interpretation of the issue is, and finally note our present General Assembly policy as it applies to this guideline.

A WARNING: In each set of guidelines, I give examples of how the church has *mis*interpreted Scripture and the Confessions. You may find this painful, as I have. However, learning requires that we recognize our mistakes and rejoice in our positive changes of mind.

THE METHOD OF THIS BOOK

In the midseventies, two educational psychologists decided to test their educational theories by observing a master teacher. The teacher they chose was John Wooden, the coach of the UCLA basketball team. Wooden had coached the UCLA basketball team to ten national championships in twelve years, a record unapproached by any other coach. During what turned out to be Wooden's last season, 1974–75, the two psychologists observed over twenty practice sessions and carefully recorded and coded each interaction Coach Wooden had with his players. Most of the interactions fit one of the standard teaching categories that they knew. One of Wooden's teaching methods was so new to them that they had to add a category. The psychologists called it a scold/reinstruction. It consisted of a criticism followed instantly by instruction on how to do the play right. When a player made a mistake, Wooden would stop the play. He would go to the player, and say, "Not like that." Then he would illustrate the correct way and say, "Do it like this." The psychologists felt that this technique was so unique and so effective that they named it a "Wooden."[2]

I am using Coach Wooden's method in this book. I first give an illustration of how the church has misinterpreted Scripture or the Confessions, and I show the unhelpful consequences of such misinterpretation. Then comes the good news. In each case I show how the church has changed its mind and become more faithful to the intent of the biblical or confessional writers. I remind us of how we developed a more adequate method of interpreting Scripture and how we have amended the Confessions or developed a new and more adequate statement of faith.

The church does make progress. It comes through the painful process of repentance, changing our minds, and correcting our practice. By observing this pattern of repentance and renewal I hope we will be better able to be faithful in our interpretation in the future.

TIMES OF CONTROVERSY

Although guidelines for studying Scripture and the Confessions are helpful for personal and devotional reading and reflection, most were designed for and are especially helpful in times of controversy in the church. Controversy surrounding the interpretation of Scripture and the Confessions has not been unusual in the church.

For example, recent disagreements regarding the appropriate sexual behavior for ordained officeholders led to placing the following sentence in the governmental standards of the church: "Persons refusing to repent of any self-acknowledged practice which the confessions call sin shall not be ordained and/or installed as deacons, elders, or ministers of the Word and Sacrament."[3] That statement is very broad in its application. It makes the definition of sin in the various ancient, Reformation, and modern Confessions a standard for judging contemporary behavior. That makes correct interpretation of the Confessions a serious and responsible task for contemporary Presbyterian Christians.

Even if we all were to follow the guidelines in this book, we would still not necessarily all think alike, nor would all of our problems automatically be solved. We would, however, be better able to talk together and be sure that we are dealing responsibly with all of the relevant issues. Having common, shared methods of interpretation would help us to be the church—in obedience to Jesus Christ, under the authority of Scripture, and guided by our confessions—when we meet difficult and potentially divisive issues. That is worth the time and effort.

After teaching in parables, Jesus said: "Let anyone with ears to hear listen!" (Mark 4:9; Luke 8:8). His disciples often asked him to interpret the meaning of his teaching (Matthew 13:36). Our goal is to be those with ears to hear Jesus and to interpret our sources of authority and guidance according to his teaching.

Part One

INTERPRETING AN
AUTHORITATIVE SCRIPTURE

The wisdom of God hath so tempered the Scriptures, as that from thence the wisest Solomon may fetch jewels for ornament, and the poorest Lazarus, bread for life. . . . It is true, there are . . . hard things, to exercise the study and diligence, the faith and prayers of the profoundest scholars; waters wherein an elephant may swim . . . but every one who hath the Spirit of Christ, hath therewith a judgment to discern so much of God's will, as shall suffice to make him believe in Christ for righteousness, and, by worship and obedience, to serve him unto salvation.

—Edward Reynolds, a principal author of the Westminster
Confession of Faith, writing of Scripture in 1645[1]

1

Everyone Interprets

We all, each day, interpret what we read, view, and experience. For example, we read newspapers and interpret the news sections differently than we do the editorial sections. We watch television and interpret a sitcom differently than we do a weather forecast. We go to the movies, and we interpret a romantic comedy differently than we do a documentary on dangers to our environment. We go to church, and we interpret the announcements of the coming week's activities differently than we do the exhortation to spiritual growth in the sermon. We do all of this quite automatically, without being aware of it.[1]

We are all interpreters of the various kinds of communications that we receive daily. We are not even aware that we are interpreting, unless or until we discover that we have misinterpreted something. Remember how, back in 1938 when Orson Welles did his now famous radio broadcast *The War of the Worlds*, some people panicked, believing it was a news broadcast and that we had been invaded from outer space. Today, in a different situation, someone might explain to us after church that what we took to be a serious point the minister meant as a joke.

The scholarly word for interpretation is *hermeneutics*. It comes from the Greek word meaning "to explain" or "to translate."[2] In reality, we all have been doing hermeneutics every day of our lives without knowing it.

EARLY CHRISTIAN INTERPRETATION

For the earliest Christians, biblical interpretation was essential because their Bible was the First Testament, what we call the

Old Testament. They did not yet have the Second, or New, Testament. The Hebrew Bible was their authoritative revelation from God, and they interpreted it as telling them that Jesus was the promised Messiah and Savior of the world.[3]

The early Christians therefore rejected literalism as a means of interpreting the Bible. As a result, they could ignore the comments of various dissenting groups. The Jews, for instance, said: Take the Bible literally; it doesn't say anything about Jesus! The Marcionites, who disdained the Old Testament, took it literally, as did the Gnostics, who claimed to have secret and superior wisdom. Nevertheless, the early Christians refused to treat the Bible with a superficial literalism.

Nor would the early Christians allow fanciful, subjective interpretations of Scripture. They rejected, for example, claims to direct, private revelations from God. They knew, instead, that individual claims to divine knowledge were subject to the interpretation of the church.[4]

Christians had to ground their claims to Jesus as the revelation of God in the text of the Bible as they had it. Thus they had to interpret it. So interpretation has been a Christian task from the beginning.

For the early Christians, and for us, interpreting the Bible is not just a matter of understanding what the words say or even what they mean. It is also a matter of responding appropriately to them. In John 8:31, Jesus says to the Jews who had believed in him: "If you continue in my word, you are truly my disciples; and you will know the truth, and the truth will make you free." The apostle John in a final word to his flock gently exhorted them: "Little children, let us love, not in word or speech, but in truth and action" (1 John 3:18). True interpreting is a matter of both knowing and doing the will of God.

So we need to pay attention not only to the words but to the meaning, and we need to respond appropriately to demonstrate that we have truly understood. Again, we all do this all of the time, usually without reflecting on the process. We interpret and respond differently to an advertisement on television that says "You should go to your automobile dealership right now while this special sale is on" than to a spouse who says "I hope we can spend some special time together tonight."

INTERPRETATION IN THE
REFORMED TRADITION

Some theories regarding the authority and interpretation of the Bible correspond neither to what the Bible says about itself nor to the way devout and intelligent Christian readers actually use it. And "use" is important, for the classic text about the authority of the Bible, 2 Timothy 3:16–17, emphasizes the *usefulness* of the Bible: "All scripture is inspired by God and is useful for teaching, for reproof, for correction, and for training in righteousness, so that everyone who belongs to God may be proficient, equipped for every good work."

The first principle of interpretation is to be clear as to the function of Scripture. In reading Scripture, our practice is sometimes better than our theory. For example, we recognize that much of the book of Revelation is mystical and metaphorical even when some television preachers claim that it gives us a precise blueprint for future political events. By the grace of God and the leading of the Spirit, we learn to use Scripture in the way that God intends us to—that is, for two practical purposes: (1) coming to salvation in Jesus Christ; and (2) living the Christian life.

Salvation and service are the two purposes for which we come to the Bible for guidance. When we use the Bible for other purposes we often get into trouble. Some theories about the Bible tempt us to use the Bible in ways for which it was not intended. I could use my watch for driving a nail into a board. That might work, but it would break the watch. Watches are meant for telling time, not hammering nails. Along that same line, in the seventeenth century, Irish Anglican Archbishop James Ussher counted backwards using the years the patriarchs lived, as stated in the Old Testament, to conclude that the world was created in 4004 B.C. A better understanding of Hebrew culture helps us to realize that the numbers are given not so that we can calculate the beginning of the world, but to know that the Creator is good from the very beginning and continues to care for people during all the years of their lives.

The Reformed Confessions are very clear about this twofold purpose of Scripture. The Confessions are affirmations of faith by those who have preceded us in living the Christian life from a perspective similar to ours as Presbyterians. Let us look at several examples from our foreparents in the faith that reiterate this dual purpose of Scripture.

The French Confession of 1559, recommended for study by the General Assembly, was quite directly influenced by Calvin. It states that the Bible contains "all that is necessary for the service of God and for our salvation."[5]

The Second Helvetic (Swiss) Confession of 1566 states the twofold purpose of Scripture clearly by affirming that the Bible "has the most complete exposition of all that pertains to a saving faith, and also to the framing of a life acceptable to God."[6]

The Westminster Confession of Faith, completed in 1647, says that the Bible gives us "that knowledge of God, and of his will, which is necessary unto salvation" and as such is the "rule of faith and life."[7]

The Confession of 1967 puts the same twofold purpose into contemporary language: "God's reconciling work in Jesus Christ and the mission of reconciliation to which he has called his church are the heart of the gospel in any age."[8]

A Brief Statement of Faith begins with the motif of salvation, saying, "In life and in death we belong to God."[9] Near the end it emphasizes the motif of service: "In gratitude to God, empowered by the Spirit, we strive to serve Christ in our daily tasks and to live holy and joyful lives."[10]

The Reformed Confessions are unanimous in directing us to this twofold use of Scripture: To bring us to salvation in Jesus Christ; To guide us in living a life of Christian faith. They help us realize that the first use of Scripture—salvation—is clear, and that in the second—service—we sometimes encounter religious controversies whose solution is less than clear.

2

Presbyterian Policy
on Interpreting Scripture

What do Presbyterians believe about the Bible? Presbyterians have a very orthodox, official position on the authority and interpretation of the Bible! When we speak of a Presbyterian "policy" we usually think of a social policy, an attitude toward, for instance, abortion, the environment, or women's rights. Actually, any position that a General Assembly adopts is the church's policy, unless and until another Assembly adopts a different position on the issue, in which case the policy of the church changes.

In 1982 and 1983 our predecessor denominations, the United Presbyterian Church in the United States of America (hereafter UPCUSA) and the Presbyterian Church in the United States (hereafter PCUS), adopted policy statements on the authority and interpretation of the Bible. Each denomination had a task force that for several years studied the issue of biblical interpretation. The task forces communicated with each other, and in the end the two reports and their adopted guidelines were intentionally complementary. These statements remain our "official" policy on Scripture. The two reports that gave the rationale for the policy recommendations were entitled: "Biblical Authority and Interpretation" (UPCUSA, 1982), and "Presbyterian Understanding and Use of Holy Scripture" (PCUS, 1983).[1]

The 1982 report and recommendations in "Biblical Authority and Interpretation" (UPCUSA) came about in this way. In 1976, the UPCUSA General Assembly in Baltimore authorized a Committee on Pluralism. (The same Assembly also

began the discussion on homosexuality that has continued for
the last twenty-plus years.) The purpose of the committee was
"to find out why Presbyterians fight with each other so much."[2]
Its method of research was to interview all living past modera-
tors, General Assembly staff, and other church leaders. After it
had done so, the committee concluded, in 1978:

> Widely differing views on the ways the Old and New Testa-
> ments are accepted, interpreted, and applied were repeatedly
> cited to us by lay people, clergy, and theologians as the most
> prevalent cause of conflict in our denomination today. . . . It is
> our opinion that until our church examines this problem, our
> denomination will continue to be impeded in its mission and
> ministry, or we will spiral into a destructive schism.[3]

The last statement proved to be predictive. Between 1979
and 1981 approximately sixty churches left the UPCUSA.
Most of these churches claimed a higher view of biblical authority as the reason for leaving.

In 1978 the General Assembly in San Diego responded to
this report (and the one on homosexuality) by establishing a
twelve-member Task Force on Biblical Authority and Interpretation. A few months later in 1978, the PCUS established a
parallel Task Force on Presbyterian Understanding and Use of
Holy Scripture. I was a member of the UPCUSA task force,
which met ten times over the next four years. Our group reported to the UPCUSA General Assembly in 1982 in Hartford,
Connecticut. The report was received and the guidelines were
adopted. The PCUS report came to the PCUS General Assembly in Atlanta in 1983 and was adopted just before the reunion of the UPCUSA and the PCUS was consummated.

The Theology and Worship Ministry Unit of the reunited
denomination, the Presbyterian Church (U.S.A.) [hereafter
PC (USA)] gathered the two reports into one booklet in 1992
with the following comment: "The two papers were written in
response to the need for a common basis in a diverse church
for understanding and using Scripture."[4] I will use the outline
of the UPCUSA report here because its seven guidelines are
somewhat more succinct. The PCUS report, coming later,

elaborated upon and gave helpful background to the principles of biblical interpretation contained in the earlier report. I will note those elaborations at the appropriate points.

WHAT PRESBYTERIANS BELIEVE ABOUT THE BIBLE

The UPCUSA task force, convened in 1978, was given three tasks. The first was to study the diverse ways in which Presbyterians understood biblical authority and interpretation. The second task was to describe the principles of biblical interpretation in the Reformed tradition, especially in our confessional standards. The third task was to develop guidelines for the positive use of Scripture in times of controversy.

First we were to find out what Presbyterians thought about the Bible. To accomplish this we conducted a survey through the research arm of the denomination. The "Presbyterian Panel" is a scientifically designed national sampling of Presbyterians that takes account of all of the population demographics. Each month it sends a questionnaire on a particular subject to a selected sampling of Presbyterians. Because the persons being questioned have agreed to participate, the panel usually achieves an over 80 percent response. Thus it enjoys a high degree of accuracy in its findings.

In 1980, the task force used the panel to fulfill our first mandate. Over three thousand people selected by the panel were presented with five positions on biblical authority and asked to indicate with which position they were most in agreement. The positions were written to describe views ranging from the most conservative to the most liberal.

Position 1 was a position usually known as biblical inerrancy. It read: "The Bible, though written by individuals, has been so controlled by the Holy Spirit that it is without error in all it teaches in matters of science and history as well as in matters of theology."

Position 2 also emphasized the divine element in Scripture, but was more cautious: "The Bible, though written by individuals and reflecting their personalities, has been so controlled by the Holy

Spirit that it is trustworthy in matters of theology and ethics, but not necessarily in matters of science and history."

Position 3 accepted the mystery of the uniting of the divine and human in Scripture: "All of the Bible is both the inspired word of God and at the same time a thoroughly human document."

Position 4 asserted: "Portions of the Bible, including some of its theological and ethical positions, may not be the inspired word of God." (Positions 4 and 5 moved increasingly in the direction of emphasizing the human element in the Bible.)

Position 5 alleged: "The Bible is merely a record of the moral and religious experiences of Hebrews and Christians."

Eighty-one percent of those surveyed responded. The results of the panel survey displayed a bell-shaped curve. We discovered that 48 percent of Presbyterians chose Position 3, the middle position; 82 percent held one of the three centrist views (Positions 2, 3, and 4); 85 percent held positions from the center to the more conservative side (Positions 3, 2, and 1).[5]

The center position, Position 3, affirmed what the church has always affirmed, that the Bible is both divine and human. The other positions attempt to explain the weighting and the relationship of the divine and human factors. Position 1 so emphasizes the divine factor in Scripture as virtually to eliminate the human element. Position 5 emphasizes the human factor to such an extent as almost to exclude any element of the divine. We learned that the largest number of Presbyterians were content to affirm the mystery of a Word of God that is also a human word.

The centrist group in the church (almost) always has the majority of votes in the General Assembly. At the same time, however, history teaches us that sometimes small groups, or even individuals, who are out of harmony with the majority may be pointing us to where the church must eventually move. It is especially noteworthy that nearly half of the respondents reported that they had changed positions during their lifetime. The most common change was from Positions 1 and 2 in the direction of Positions 2 and 3, that is, from a more conservative position to a more moderate position.[6]

As we will see, the church has sometimes been so captive to the surrounding culture that most good, intelligent, and devout people were unable to recognize a dominating misinterpretation of Scripture and the Confessions. Three such instances, which we will examine, are the church's attitudes toward slavery and segregation, the role of women, and divorce and remarriage. Each of these situations suggests that we must be continually open to a dialogue that involves the whole church and all of its members.

AMERICAN UNDERSTANDINGS OF THE REFORMED TRADITION

The second mandate of the task force was to explore the theological heritage of the Reformed tradition and analyze the confessional standards that should guide Presbyterians' interpretation of Scripture. Panelists were asked to identify which of the five interpretive positions listed earlier they believed was closest to the Reformed (Calvinistic Protestant) position. The responses were not necessarily theologically identical with their previous responses.

There was apparently a sense of alienation from the Reformed tradition among many of those surveyed. Half of the respondents—those holding Positions 1 through 3—claimed that their position was Reformed. Persons holding Positions 4 and 5 acknowledged that they were at a distance from the Reformed center. One-third of the respondents did not know what the phrase "Reformed Tradition" meant. Another one-third of all the panelists felt that their view was *not* Reformed![7] If two-thirds of Presbyterians do not understand or feel that they are not in accord with the Reformed tradition, we have a tremendous teaching job to do. A Brief Statement of Faith, written in 1991, and the Catechisms, sent to the church in 1998, offer hopeful resources that can present the historic Reformed tradition in present-day language and thought forms.

The situation is further complicated by the fact that, as the task force described it, in the Presbyterian church there has been over the last two centuries three significantly different understandings of biblical authority and interpretation. Each of these different understandings, or methods, was viewed in its own time as the true representative of the Reformed tradition.

How can this situation be explained? What exactly were these interpretive traditions? The task force report labeled them A, B, and C. I have given them names sometimes used in theological discussion. None of these names is universally accepted, and I mean none in any pejorative sense. They are attempts to identify what are discernibly different approaches to biblical interpretation. The first method I will call Scholastic, the second Neo-Orthodox, and the third Contextual.

The Scholastic Model:
The Bible as a Book of Inerrant Facts (1812–1927)

Two people most clearly shaped the early American Reformed view of the Bible—Francis Turretin and Thomas Reid. Both were active in the Post-Reformation period rather than in the Protestant Reformation itself. The word *Scholasticism* derives from the style of doing theology in the Middle Ages that made heavy use of philosophical methods to provide a logical, precise, and ordered system of theology. Post-Reformation Scholasticism in the seventeenth century in Europe displayed similar characteristics. Whereas Calvin, Luther, and the sixteenth-century theologians were creative biblical theologians who sought fresh insights from Scripture, their seventeenth-century continental followers, of whom Turretin is the most notable, were concerned to create a philosophically certain system of thought.[8]

Turretin's Theology

Francis Turretin taught theology in Geneva in the late seventeenth century, over one hundred years after Calvin and a decade after the Westminster Confession of Faith was written in a very different setting in England. Turretin tried to "prove" the inerrancy of the Bible in response to the Roman Catholic Counter-Reformation claim of papal infallibility. He tried to establish that the Bible was a perfect literary document in response to radical critics who argued that the Bible's demonstrably human imperfection negated its divine status.

Turretin modeled his approach not on Calvin but on Thomas Aquinas, the greatest of the medieval Roman Catholic theologians. Following Aquinas's methods of logic, Turretin tried to prove that the Scriptures were true. Calvin had specifically called such an approach "foolishness," arguing that only by the Holy Spirit working in one's heart can the authority of Scripture be known.[9] Turretin's method, following Aquinas, presumed that one should not believe anything unless it could be proved true by evidence and logic. By contrast, Calvin's method assumed that God, in grace, had planted faith in the Christian believer's heart. Building on that faith, the Christian could go on to greater understanding. Aquinas's method began with presumed facts, Calvin's with implanted faith. Aquinas (and Turretin) emphasized reason; Calvin accentuated grace.

In his quest for human certainty, Turretin went so far as to declare that even the vowel points in the Hebrew text of the Old Testament were inspired. The problem with this is that there are no vowel points in the *original* Hebrew manuscripts. The vowel points were added later to help non-Jews pronounce the Hebrew.

Turretin's rationalistic effort to *prove* the authority of Scripture happened after the development of the Westminster Confession of Faith in England. The Westminster Divines (a seventeenth-century term for ministers) had fought against the same kind of medieval methods of logic, represented in their case by the High-Church Royalists. Rather than seeking secular proof to make belief possible, they followed Calvin in assuming that faith led to understanding.[10]

Scottish Common Sense Philosophy

Thomas Reid was a Presbyterian minister and philosopher in Scotland. Reid responded, as did most religious thinkers in the eighteenth century, to the rise of empirical science, that is, to the belief that knowledge comes from our senses and from the application of precise scientific measurements. Isaac Newton's notion of a rigidly fixed mechanical universe had become so generally acknowledged that it was applied to all of life, including both science and religion. In fact, the word *inerrant*, later applied to the Bible, was first used in English in 1652 with reference to the movement of the planets.[11]

Reid was a boring preacher but a brilliant mathematician. To the delight of his congregation, he left and became professor of mathematics at the University of Glasgow. Because mathematics and philosophy were lodged in the same university department, he also taught "moral philosophy."

Reid wanted to avoid the skepticism of philosopher David Hume, who argued that all we could know from our senses was that we are having sense experiences. This meant that nothing could be known for certain; people merely relied on custom or habit in making choices about life.

Although Reid wanted more certain knowledge than Hume allowed, Reid also wanted to be a "modern" empiricist. In his time, that meant accepting that all knowledge comes originally from our five senses: sight, hearing, touch, taste, and smell. In response to this challenge, Reid developed a theory known as "Scottish Realism," or "Scottish Common Sense Philosophy." To do this, Reid linked his religious beliefs and his scientific assumptions. He declared that our senses are completely reliable guides to all knowledge. When asked how he knew that, Reid asserted that we have in our hearts an intuition (like a religious conviction) that our senses are completely reliable.

Common Sense Philosophy took Scotland by storm. It was egalitarian. All people could make their own judgments without need of experts. And it allowed two things. First, Reid's Common Sense Philosophy allowed everyone to be a scientist, for it claimed that our senses give us complete and reliable information about objects in nature. Second, because Reid assumed that all people everywhere think alike, everyone can know exactly what everyone else thinks. We can, for example, know what the apostle Paul meant without any knowledge or study of ancient languages or culture. There are no problems of interpretation. The truth is obvious.

The popularity of Common Sense Philosophy moved beyond the boundaries of Scotland to America. Thomas Jefferson, for example, met a disciple of Reid, Dugald Stewart, in Paris and was enthralled by this democratic philosophy. In fact, the first words of the Declaration of Independence—"We hold these truths to be *self-evident*"—agree with Scottish Common Sense Philosophy.

The Scot John Witherspoon, a signer of the Declaration of Independence, brought Scottish Common Sense Philosophy to the College of New Jersey (later, Princeton University) when he became its president in 1768. Common Sense Philosophy became the accepted viewpoint in many of America's earliest colleges and universities.[12] Take the case of Princeton Seminary, formed as an independent theological training institution in 1812. Its curriculum, chosen by its first professor, Archibald Alexander, was based, not on the writings of Calvin or the Divines who wrote the Westminster Confession of Faith, but on Turretin's systematic theology and Reid's Common Sense Philosophy. These influences were at the heart of Princeton Seminary's early teachings about biblical interpretation.[13]

Princeton had widespread influence on generations of Presbyterians, and as a result most influential nineteenth- and early twentieth-century Presbyterian theologians in America were dedicated followers of Turretin and Scottish Common Sense Philosophy. Charles Hodge, his son Archibald Alexander Hodge, and his successor Benjamin Breckenridge Warfield taught this philosophical theology at Princeton Seminary into the 1920s. In the South during this same time, the leading theologians James Henley Thornwell and Robert Lewis Dabney were equally committed to the Scottish Common Sense approach.

The Nineteenth-Century
Interpretation of Westminster

All of the influential teachers of theology at Princeton Seminary, in the North, and Union and Columbia, in the South, attributed their view of Scripture to the Westminster Confession. Indeed, Warfield wrote: "It is our special felicity that, as Reformed Christians and heirs of the richest and fullest formulation of Reformed thought, we possess in that precious heritage, the Westminster Confession, the most complete, the most admirable, the most perfect statement of the essential Christian doctrine of Holy Scripture which has ever been formed by man."[14] The actual sources they used for their theology were, however, Turretin's late seventeenth-century worldview and Reid's eighteenth-century understanding of science.

Charles Hodge, in words similar to those of his southern col-
league, Thornwell, said: "The Bible is to the theologian what
nature is to the man of science. It is his storehouse of facts."[15]
With Turretin's system and Reid's method of interpretation,
these theologians understood the Bible to contain a logical system of divinely chosen words. It was therefore inerrant in all
things, including science and history. Warfield believed that
the Bible was in harmony with the results of nineteenth-
century science, and he taught just that.[16]

This view intended reverence for the authority of the
Bible. The Bible was claimed to be the judge over all human
thought and could not be judged by humans.[17] Unfortunately, its eighteenth- and nineteenth-century practitioners
did not realize that they were imposing a human system on
Scripture that was, in many ways, not in harmony with the
very character of Scripture. Inevitable conflicts occurred between this older view and the newer literary and historical
study of the Bible that began in the late nineteenth and early
twentieth centuries.

For our purposes, here, it is important to remember that
this rationalistic method of interpreting the Bible was incor-
rectly attributed to the Westminster Confession. Generations
of students were led to believe that they were imbibing the
view of the Westminster Divines, when they were actually
studying Turretin or Hodge or Thornwell or Dabney in the
classroom. This helps us to understand why later generations—in response to new methods of interpretation—felt
they had to reject the Westminster Confession. They were
trying merely to move beyond the influence of the Old Princeton approach to the Bible, but that approach had become identified completely with the Westminster Confession of Faith.

The Presbyterian Church U.S.A. never formally rejected the
Old Princeton theory about the Bible. In 1927, after decades of
the Fundamentalist/Modernist controversy over the domi-
nance of the Old Princeton position, the General Assembly in
effect set it aside by refusing to allow General Assembly interpretations of the Westminster Confession to have the force of
church law.[18] However, the nineteenth-century Princeton po-

sition is still considered by some Presbyterians to be the most authentic Reformed approach to Scripture because they believe it to be rooted in the teachings of the Westminster Confession of Faith.[19]

Now we need to turn to the second model of Reformed interpretation that has prevailed in American Presbyterianism.

Neo-Orthodoxy:
The Bible as a Witness to Christ,
the Word of God (1930s–1960s)

Just as the Fundamentalist/Modernist controversy was concluding in the 1930s, the fresh theological breeze of Neo-Orthodoxy blew in from Europe. It was called "Neo" because it was a *new* approach that was not dependent on either Protestant Scholasticism nor its liberal opponents. It was "Orthodox" in that it turned people's attention to Jesus Christ as revealed in Scripture and depended on the work of the Holy Spirit to make the biblical message alive through preaching. Neo-Orthodoxy focused on the traditional doctrines of the Christian faith but looked at them afresh in the light of current scholarship. The movement was also called Neo-Calvinism, Neo-Protestantism, and Neo-Reformation theology.[20] The names of Swiss Neo-Orthodox theologians Karl Barth and Emil Brunner became common in American theological schools in the 1940s and 1950s.[21]

Worldwide economic depression, the rise of totalitarian governments, and the use of science to produce weapons of mass destruction in two world wars had dashed the previous liberal optimism about human nature. Human effort was not bringing in God's kingdom, nor was human reason proving adequate to know God. Neo-orthodoxy's defining insight, taken from the Danish philosopher Søren Kierkegaard, was that persons and God are known by personal encounter, not by rational procedures.[22] The revelation of God comes not in an inspired book, but in the person of Jesus Christ, who is God incarnate.[23]

Thus, the Bible is a witness to Christ. To make this point, Barth hung over his desk a print of Mattheus Grunewald's

Ishenheim altarpiece from Colmar, France. In it, John the Baptist, symbolizing the role of the Bible, stands pointing a long, bony finger at Christ on the cross. Because the Bible, like John the Baptist, points away from itself to Christ, the issue of possible mistakes in the Bible is irrelevant. By the actions of the Holy Spirit, through preaching, the Bible *becomes* the word of God to persons of faith.

The Confession of 1967 reflects this emphasis, beginning its section on the Bible with the statement: "The one sufficient revelation of God is Jesus Christ, the Word of God incarnate, to whom the Holy Spirit bears unique and authoritative witness through the Holy Scriptures, which are received and obeyed as the word of God written."[24]

The Confession of 1967

It was not until the 1960s that Presbyterians were able to give confessional expression to the Neo-Orthodox insights regarding Scripture that had been developed in the 1940s. In 1956 the Presbytery of Amarillo (PCUSA) overtured the General Assembly, requesting that the Westminster Shorter Catechism be rewritten in contemporary language. The Assembly appointed a committee, chaired by Arthur Adams of Rochester, New York, to deal with this request. In 1957, the Adams Committee proposed two alternatives:

1. That a committee be appointed to prepare a historical introduction to the Shorter Catechism and revise the Scripture references attached to it. Or:
2. That a committee be named to draft "a brief contemporary statement of faith to be included in the Constitution after the union is consummated in 1958."

(A brief aside on the issue of union: The Presbyterian Church, U.S.A. [PCUSA] and the United Presbyterian Church in North America [UPNA] effected a merger in 1958 after an attempted three-way union, including the Presbyterian Church in the United States [PCUS], failed in 1954. This merged

Northern church was named the United Presbyterian Church in the United States of America [UPCUSA].)

The second alternative was preferred by the committee, whose rationale was that "it should bring to all members of our Church some sense of participation in the thrilling revival of theology." That thrilling revival was, of course, the Neo-Orthodox consensus that had begun to develop in the early 1940s and continued still.[25]

When, in 1958, the UPNA merged with the PCUSA to form the UPCUSA, the 1925 doctrinal statement of the UPNA was set aside. It stated that "the Scriptures of the Old and New Testaments are the Word of God and are inspired throughout, in language as well as thought."[26] The merged denomination accepted only the Westminster Confession of Faith and Catechisms as its doctrinal base.

At the uniting General Assembly in 1958, a Committee on a Brief Contemporary Statement of Faith was named. Nine men were appointed to the committee, with Edward A. Dowey, Jr., of Princeton Theological Seminary, as chair. Over the next four years, eleven more members were added to the committee, including one woman, ruling elder Mrs. E. Harris Harbison. The theology of most of the members of the committee had been shaped by the Neo-Orthodox revival of the 1940s and 1950s.

In 1959 the committee returned to the General Assembly and requested a broader mandate. In 1964, the Assembly gave final approval to a revised threefold focus for the committee's work. The final document was to contain: (1) a book of creeds and confessions; (2) a contemporary statement that was a confession of the meaning of Christ's reconciling work concretely in the life of the church rather than a syllabus of all the topics in theology; (3) appropriate changes in the ordination questions for church officers.

The Confession of 1967 and the Westminster Confession

The committee mistakenly identified the view of Scripture in the Westminster Confession as identical with that of the Old Princeton literalistic inerrancy approach. That was understandable, of course, given the 150-year history of that identification by the dominant theological party in the Presbyterian church. Dowey, Arnold Come, and others on the committee who had studied at Princeton near the end of the Old Princeton era in the early 1940s knew the inadequacy of that older tradition. They had felt rescued and renewed by the theological thought of European Neo-Orthodox theologians such as Emil Brunner and Joseph Hromadka, who had lectured at Princeton. Committee members were determined to rid the church of the rigidifying influence of Old Princeton that they identified with the Westminster Confession.

The committee believed that only Neo-Orthodoxy could save the Scriptures from the ravages of literary criticism. Revelation in the person of Jesus Christ, not the inspiration of a book, was what mattered. Neo-Orthodoxy would also save the Scriptures from the Old Princeton doctrine of inerrancy, which the committee equated with the doctrine of the Westminster Confession of Faith. The explanatory section on "the Place of the Bible" in the "Introductory Comment and Analysis" to the Confession of 1967 made it clear: "This section is an intended revision of the Westminster doctrine, which rested primarily on a view of inspiration and equated the biblical canon directly with the Word of God. By contrast, the preeminent and primary meaning of the Word of God in the Confession of 1967 is the Word of God incarnate."[27] The committee report concluded with a more detailed discussion of interpretation: "Questions of antiquated cosmology, diverse cultural influences and the like, may be dealt with by careful scholarship uninhibited by the doctrine of inerrancy which placed the older Reformed theology at odds with advances in historical and scientific studies."[28] Scripture should not be equated with the Word of God but be understood as a normative witness to Christ, the Word of God.

In 1965, following the presentation of proposed confessional changes, a Special Committee of Fifteen was established by the General Assembly to receive responses to the report and consider amendments. Independent organizations of ministers and laypersons were convened to advocate for changes in the proposed contemporary confession. A vigorous two-year debate took place. The General Assembly mandated a revision committee that had the power to rewrite the initial draft. This committee received eleven hundred letters recommending changes.

The Bible in the Confession of 1967

The final version of the section on Scripture in the Confession of 1967 was a compromise between those who wanted to speak only of Jesus Christ as the Word of God and those who also insisted on speaking of Scripture as the Word of God. The final draft read: "The one sufficient revelation of God is Jesus Christ, the Word of God incarnate, to whom the Holy Spirit bears unique and authoritative witness through the Holy Scriptures, which are received and obeyed as the word of God written." A capital *W* was used to designate Christ as the Word of God, whereas a lowercase *w* was used for word of God in reference to Scripture.[29]

The great values of Neo-Orthodoxy are three: (1) It directs our attention to Christ as the primary revelation of God; (2) It deflects the attention from the literary controversies that were prominent during the Fundamentalist/Modernist controversy and allows people to both affirm the authority of the Bible and be open to scholarly analysis of it as a historical and literary document; (3) It enables us to get beyond using ancient, culturally conditioned texts as contemporary universal laws. Rather, we are enabled to view social problems through the lens of the total teaching and practice of the divine/human person, Jesus Christ.

By the time the Confession of 1967 was adopted, however, academic support for Neo-Orthodoxy was waning. New issues, not addressed by Neo-orthodoxy, became prominent: the resurgence of science; religious, racial, and ethnic pluralism; the rise of non–Euro-American concerns; and, in the 1970s, the struggle for the equality of women. All the great Neo-Orthodox theologians had died, and no one with a similar perspective had taken their place to address these concerns.[30]

In response to this changing environment, a third model of biblical interpretation gradually developed in the Presbyterian church.[31]

Contextual Biblical Interpretation:
A Divine Message in Human Forms
of Thought (1970s–1980s)

Contextual theology takes seriously the human, social location of the biblical writings and the influence of our own history and culture on our methods of interpretation. Theological formulations are developed in context, not only from what the Bible says but also from felt needs of theologians and their perceptions of reality in the world around them. Jesus Christ, it is argued, by becoming incarnate in a certain place and time voluntarily accepted the limitations of that worldly setting. So, in interpreting the Bible we must take account of the human setting in which God dealt with people and be conscious of the way in which our own social location has shaped our ability to understand and interpret the biblical message.[32]

Historical research on Calvin and the sixteenth-century Reformers, begun during the Neo-Orthodox period, did not stop with the waning of Neo-Orthodoxy. A consensus emerged, for example, that Calvin was not the inerrantist depicted by the Old Princeton tradition of Hodge and Warfield; nor was he the existentialist described by the early Neo-Orthodox theologians. Early in his career, Barth had followed the insight of the Danish philosopher Søren Kierkegaard that Christ was known by a "leap of faith," that is, by personal commitment rather than by rational objectivity.[33] A new model of interpretation was needed that took into account additional insights into how Calvin and the other sixteenth-century Reformers actually used the Bible.

In response, scholars now began to emphasize an incarnational, or contextual, understanding of Scripture's function. In this view, the Bible was certainly an inspired book (more than some of Barth's followers had thought it was), but it was also a collection of humanly written documents (more than Hodge and Warfield had acknowledged). People increasingly realized that the more we understand about the human origins of the biblical documents, the better we can understand the divine message contained in them.[34]

The Bible showed evidence that God had accommodated, or condescended, or adapted God's own understanding to our limited human means of comprehension. Early church theologians such as Origen (A.D. 185–254) and Augustine (A.D. 354–430) used the imagery of God as a parent or teacher to convey that God, the person of greater knowledge, willingly limited and adapted himself to the lesser knowledge of human beings so that we could adequately know God in our own human way. Origen, the first theologian of the early church, said, and Calvin later affirmed, that God talks "baby talk." Calvin said, "God is wont in a measure to 'lisp' in speaking to us," like nursemaids do with infants.[35]

Calvin was bold to say that we do not know God "as he is in himself, but as he seems to us."[36] This attitude reflected Isaiah's reminder that God's thoughts are not our thoughts, nor are God's ways our ways (Isa. 55:8). Because God came to us in the human person of Jesus Christ and in the human language of the Bible, we as human beings can understand God adequately enough to come into a saving relation with God and to live as Christian people in this world.

That is the divine function of the incarnation of Christ and of the Bible—to bring us into a right relationship with God. This approach, which stressed the human context of the biblical writings and their function of bringing people into relationship to God, seemed to be the consensus of a group of prominent Reformed scholars in the 1980s, including Ford Lewis Battles, the translator of Calvin's *Institutes*, British theologian and historian T. H. L. Parker, and the Dutch theologian G. C. Berkouwer.

The values of this approach to biblical interpretation are numerous. It provided: (1) the opportunity to take seriously the insights of the social sciences of psychology, sociology, and anthropology in understanding the human manner in which the writers of Scripture communicated their message; (2) the ability to take seriously the cultural context of the ancient Near East as the matrix in which the biblical material has been formed; and (3) a recognition that human, relational metaphors, rather than scientific or propositional statements, best describe the manner of God's communication with people in Scripture.[37]

Confusion, and even conflict, over the Reformed method of biblical interpretation is understandable given these three

different approaches, each of which has had widespread support in American Presbyterian history. Contemporary approaches to biblical interpretation can draw on values
imbedded in each of the three historical movements. The intended reverence for the Bible's authority emphasized in the
Scholastic approach makes us take the Bible seriously. The
Neo-Orthodoxy model helpfully points us to the living Word
of God, Jesus Christ, as the primary revelation of God. The
contemporary Contextual style allows us to take full account of
human cultural context through which the divine message
comes. We are also more aware of the influence of our own social location upon the way we approach Scripture.

We can learn from each of these three historical approaches,
but none, taken alone, is fully adequate for our present needs.
Thus the Presbyterian church has developed and adopted a series of guidelines that will enable us to focus on the most important factors in understanding the Bible's message to us.

3

Seven Guidelines for Interpreting Scripture in Matters of Controversy

Guidelines adopted in 1982 and elaborated upon with the merger that formed the PC(USA) in 1983 are still relevant and useful. In this chapter I will cite each of seven guidelines and then briefly explain their meaning. I note in each case connections between the contemporary guideline and other, similar principles found in the PC(USA) *Book of Confessions.* There is confessional confirmation of each guideline because they were originally drawn from a study of our Reformed confessional heritage. Finally, I will indicate what I consider some practical consequences of each of the guidelines. These will highlight some of the reasons why careful and thoughtful interpretation of the Scriptures matters in our everyday lives.

It is important to note that these guidelines are meant to be taken collectively. Together they give us a framework for approaching Scripture in a wholesome manner. They provide checks and balances so that no one perspective will distort our perception of the truth of Scripture. To take only one principle of interpretation to the exclusion of others has often caused dissension and even division in the church. Controversy in the church could be lessened if we all used this constellation of denominationally approved guidelines for biblical interpretation.[1]

1. RECOGNIZE THAT JESUS CHRIST, THE REDEEMER, IS THE CENTER OF SCRIPTURE.

The Bible is a story with a central character, Jesus Christ. The Bible is more like a novel or a play than an encyclopedia. It has a plot, a story line. That story is a very simple one that characterizes the Christian faith: A good God made a good Creation. Human creatures sinned and became alienated from God. God did not leave us alone, but came in the person of Jesus Christ to restore our relationship to God. Creation, Fall, Redemption is the outline of the Christian story. Jesus Christ is the central character in that drama.

a. Confessional Confirmation

Our Reformed heritage affirms that Christ is the central interpretive principle of Scripture. Calvin, in his commentary on John 12:48 says: "In our reading of Scripture we shall hold simply to that which speaks clearly and definitely to our conscience and makes us feel that it leads us to Christ."[2]

The Scots Confession says: "When controversy arises about the right understanding of any passage or sentence of Scripture, or for the reformation of any abuse within the Kirk of God, we ought not so much to ask what men have said or done before us, as what the Holy Ghost uniformly speaks within the body of Scriptures and what Christ Jesus himself did and commanded."[3]

From the Theological Declaration of Barmen, written against Hitler in 1934, comes this memorable word: "Jesus Christ, as he is attested for us in Holy Scripture, is the one Word of God which we have to hear and which we have to trust and obey in life and in death."[4]

Our American Confession of 1967 states clearly: "The Bible is to be interpreted in light of its witness to God's work of reconciliation in Christ."[5]

b. Practical Consequences

What is the practical value of reflecting on Christ as the center of Scripture? One example will no doubt stimulate you to think of many others.

When we recognize Christ as the center of Scripture, we must also recognize that Jesus' teaching and attitudes should be used to interpret the Pauline teachings, not the other way around. In the 1950s, Westminster Press produced an interesting and helpful trilogy of books: *The Case for Theology in Liberal Perspective; The Case for a New Reformation Theology;* and *The*

Case for Orthodox Theology. This last volume was authored by Edward John Carnell of Fuller Theological Seminary and published in 1959. It caused quite a stir because Carnell not only expounded a classic evangelical theology but also criticized fundamentalism, a movement with close ties to evangelicalism.[6] Despite its many merits, a rereading of Carnell's case for orthodox theology reminds us that its interpretive principles are inherited from the Old Princeton approach. Carnell offers the principles that (1) "the Epistles interpret the Gospels," (2) "systematic passages interpret the Incidental," (3) "universal passages interpret the local," and (4) "didactic passages interpret the symbolic." In each statement is the underlying assumption that there is a systematic theology, just below the surface of Scripture, that is the fullest expression of the Christian faith.[7]

Carnell's assumptions distort the character of the Bible. Scripture is actually a collection of many books that exhibit many different literary forms. Moreover, history demonstrates that at times systematic theology derives its system, and much of its content, from the culture of the systematician. Theologians, for example, justified slavery and the subordination of women with their culturally conditioned systems. The best corrective to such cultural conditioning is to look freshly at all of God's Word through the perspective of the living Word of God, Jesus Christ.

My wife and I sometimes do our devotional reading of Scripture following the plan for reading the Bible in a year; the plan was developed by our friend Jim Davison, at Westminster Church in Pittsburgh.[8] Reading the biblical books in course can be a refreshing alternative to the use of a lectionary. The plan requires that you read from two to three chapters of the Old Testament and a similar number of New Testament chapters each day. Because of the amount of time it takes, Sharon and I decided to read through the Bible in two years rather than one. One year we do the New Testament, and the next we do the Old Testament.

Reading only Old Testament passages makes one realize that Jesus is the best interpreter of Scripture. For example, Jesus penetrated the thicket of human rules and rituals of the Pentateuch (the first five books of the Old Testament) and identified "Love God and love your neighbor" as the essence of the law. His complete unwillingness to conform to the legalisms of his day should be instructive for us.

Slugging one's way through First and Second Kings and First and Second Chronicles at first glance does not offer much of an inspirational character. Mostly it describes kings who do every bloodthirsty thing you can think of and then are murdered by someone who tries to outdo them in doing wrong. Then you realize that at the center of the Old Testament, and the New, as Jesus interpreted them, is the basic biblical warning to beware of idolatry. Only God, the Creator, is absolute and deserves our ultimate loyalty. It is idolatry to absolutize any created thing, including our ideas and social structures. As we have observed painfully in our Presbyterian history, idolatry can include male gender, white skin color, and the married state.

Reading the prophetic books, one is struck by their continual denunciation of God's favored people when they treat others unjustly. The prophets relentlessly remind Israel of God's continual concern for the poor, the captives, the sick, and the oppressed. Then we understand Jesus' announcement of his ministry in the synagogue in Nazareth. He read from the Isaiah scroll:

> "The Spirit of the Lord is upon me,
>   because he has anointed me
>   to bring good news to the poor.
> He has sent me to proclaim release to the captives
>   and recovery of sight to the blind,
>   to let the oppressed go free,
>   to proclaim the year of the Lord's favor."[9]

Then he said, "Today this scripture has been fulfilled in your hearing." Jesus fulfilled the intent and purpose of the Old Testament. When you read Scripture regularly, you become convinced that Jesus is the best interpreter of the Bible, both Old and New Testament.

Jesus Christ is not only our Savior and Sovereign, he provides the best insights for interpreting the whole of Scripture. That is the meaning of the first principle of biblical interpretation: Jesus Christ, the Redeemer, is the center of Scripture. Just as our personal lives are redeemed by our relationship to Jesus, so also our understanding of the Bible is illumined by looking at it through Jesus' message and ministry.

2. LET THE FOCUS BE ON THE PLAIN TEXT OF SCRIPTURE.

Focus on the grammatical and historical context of Scripture. Just as principle 1 eliminates superficial literalism, this principle warns against reading into Scripture what we want it to say. One form such a misreading can take is allegorism, which was so popular in the medieval church. Allegorism looks for multiple (as many as seven) levels of meaning behind the plain meaning of the text. If we are going to deal with the Bible, we must deal with a given text as it is. If we are going to read the Bible, we must read the Bible as it is given to us, not just look for what we wish it said.

a. Confessional Confirmation

Our Reformed Confessions confirm this principle. The PCUS study of 1983 that elaborates our guidelines indicates that to do justice to the plain text we must: (1) define the appropriate literary units (passages, paragraphs, pericopes, etc.); (2) recognize the cultural conditioning of the language; and (3) understand the social and historical circumstances of the writing. This means that we say, for example: "Epic poetry is not historical chronicle; symbolic stories are not science; and admonition to a particular person or community is not general law."[10]

John Calvin declared: "There are many statements in Scripture the meaning of which depends upon their context."[11]

The Second Helvetic Confession says: "But we hold that interpretation of the Scripture to be orthodox and genuine which is gleaned . . . (from the nature of the language in which they were written, likewise according to the circumstances in which they were set down)."[12]

The Confession of 1967 says: "The Scriptures, given under the guidance of the Holy Spirit, are nevertheless the words of men, conditioned by the language, thought forms, and literary fashions of the places and times at which they are written. They reflect views of life, history, and the cosmos which were then current. The church, therefore, has an obligation to approach the Scriptures with literary and historical understanding."[13]

b. Practical Consequences

We must be careful not to ascribe divine sanction to a cultural order on the theory that because this is good in our eyes God must have intended it so. For centuries, good, intelligent, and devout Christian people believed that blacks should be enslaved by whites, that women should be subordinated to men, and that divorce disbarred one from leadership in the Christian community. Christians uncritically accepted sinful aspects of the culture of biblical times as part of the revelation of God to us. That allowed Christian people to accept sinful aspects of their own established social order and then ascribe biblical sanction to them.

C. S. Lewis, in *Reflections on the Psalms*, offers some salutary advice on this subject. In the following quotation, Lewis is referring to the Fundamentalist's view of the Bible and the Roman Catholic's view of the church:

> But there is one argument which we should beware of using for either position: God must have done what is best, this is best, therefore God has done this. For we are mortals and do not know what is best for us, and it is dangerous to prescribe what God must have done—especially when we cannot, for the life of us, see that He has after all done it.[14]

Because of our difficulty in discerning what is cultural and what is biblical, we must beware of shifting the locus of discussion from the interpretation of the Bible to some other, more general and impossible to refute issue such as the authority of the Bible, the Lordship of Christ, or the future of Western civilization. We need to stick to the plain text of Scripture and seek to understand what it originally said and what it means to us today.

For example, in 1916, the PCUS General Assembly adopted a resolution that reaffirmed statements of previous General Assemblies that both Scripture and the confessional standards prohibited women from publicly expounding God's Word from the pulpit, and that forbade women from being ordained or licensed. That was not new. However, the resolution omitted any reference to whether women could speak in what were called "promiscuous assemblies," those composed of both men and women. That was new. For the first time the issue of whether a woman could speak, for example, in the local congregational prayer meeting was left "to the discretion of our sessions and the enlightened consciences of our Christian women themselves."

It may be difficult today for us to believe that this could be a matter of great principle. However, sixty-one commissioners immediately protested this omission as a violation of biblical authority. The Assembly answered in words that have continuing relevance to us: "The Scriptures may have their authority discredited not merely by a violation of their precepts, but also by any attempt on the part of ecclesiastical courts to bind the consciences of God's people on matters of doubtful interpretation."[15]

Guideline 2, "Let the focus be on the plain text of Scripture," means that we are to take seriously the real Bible, not substitute ideas that we would prefer. To take the text seriously means that we must understand its language, the social and cultural context of its creation, and what it meant to its original intended audience. The word "plain" therefore does not mean that we can just pick up the Bible and read it as if it were written today. This guideline means to deal with the given text of the Bible in all of its complex human and divine character.

3. DEPEND UPON THE GUIDANCE OF THE HOLY SPIRIT IN INTERPRETING AND APPLYING GOD'S MESSAGE.

The same God who persuaded us of the authority of Scripture, by what Calvin called the "inner testimony of the Holy Spirit," will also aid us in interpreting Scripture. Note carefully: The Holy Spirit does not give us new information. If we haven't done our homework for the test, we must not expect the Spirit to whisper the answers in our ear. Rather, the Spirit gives us something different but all important—a receptive attitude that enables us rightly to understand and apply the message that is there in the plain text.

a. Confessional Confirmation

Our Confessions confirm this principle. The Westminster Confession: "We acknowledge the inward illumination of the Spirit of God to be necessary for the saving understanding of such things as are revealed in the Word."[16]

The Westminster Confession: "The Supreme Judge, by which all controversies of religion are to be determined, and all decrees of councils, opinions of ancient writers, doctrines of men, and private spirits, are to be examined, and in whose sentence we are to rest, can be no other but the Holy Spirit speaking in the Scripture."[17]

The Confession of 1967: "God's Word is spoken to his church today where the Scriptures are faithfully preached and attentively read in dependence on the illumination of the Holy Spirit and with readiness to receive their truth and direction."[18]

b. Practical Consequences

We need to take seriously the ongoing illumination of the biblical text by the Holy Spirit. The Holy Spirit did not cease to act at the closing of the canon when our present books of the Bible were gathered into one collection. God continues to guide us and lead us into deeper understandings of biblical truth, correcting our errors. If we had never learned anything new from Scripture since the early church, we would be incapable of living as Christians in the modern world. Great movements of church renewal, such as the modern missionary movement, were departures from past practice and were undertaken under the guidance of the Holy Spirit.

We have had to admit past mistakes under the guidance of the Holy Spirit. In 1956, a PCUS report acknowledged that "we no longer argue that human slavery is justified by the Bible, and in accord with God's will. Some of our grandfathers did so argue. . . . Through the illumination of the Holy Spirit, we have come to a different understanding on this subject." We have all benefited by that further illumination of the Spirit.[19]

We must always ask, not just what God did in a past era, on the assumption that it is definitive for all time, but rather what God is saying to the church now! In Isaiah 43:18–19 God says, "Do not remember the former things, or consider the things of old. I am about to do a new thing; now it springs forth, do you not perceive it?"[20] Jesus promised his followers that the Holy Spirit would lead them into a deeper understanding of the truth—and so the Spirit has led us.[21]

The function of the Holy Spirit is to take the things of Christ and show them to us. That means both enabling us to understand what the biblical text meant to those to whom it was originally addressed and making it possible for us to see new relevance in the text for our time. The Holy Spirit provides a creative, dynamic power in biblical interpretation. We must not cut ourselves off from the new things that God would have us learn from Scripture. The possibility of learning something new is the promise of guideline 3: depend on the guidance of the Holy Spirit in interpreting and applying God's message.

4. BE GUIDED BY THE DOCTRINAL CONSENSUS OF THE CHURCH, WHICH IS THE "RULE OF FAITH."

The amazing thing about the documents in our *Book of Confessions* is not that there are differences among them. One would expect that, given that they were written in different historical and cultural contexts. Rather, the amazing thing is the clear continuity of the Christian message over time. That is what is meant by the "rule of faith."

a. Confessional Confirmation

The Heidelberg Catechism, Question and Answer 22: Question: "What, then, must a Christian believe?" Answer: "All that is promised us in the gospel, a summary of which is taught us in the articles of the Apostles' Creed, our universally acknowledged confession of faith."[22]

Most of the Reformation era Confessions, and even the two volumes of Calvin's *Institutes*, are elaborations on the Apostles' Creed, the Ten Commandments, and the Lord's Prayer. So is the adult Study Catechism approved in 1998 by the General Assembly for use in our churches.

Our Confessions confirm the importance of referring to the doctrinal consensus of the church. The 1983 PCUS report "Presbyterian Understanding and Use of Holy Scripture" states: "Since the guidance of the Holy Spirit is promised to individual Christians for the sake of building up and equipping the community of Christians for its mission in the world, the church's consensus is likely to be more accurate than the opinions of individual persons."[23]

The Second Helvetic Confession makes the same point: "The apostle Peter has said that the Holy Scriptures are not of private interpretation (II Peter 1:20), and thus we do not allow all possible interpretations."[24] The Scriptures are always to be interpreted by and in the community of the church, the Body of Christ.

b. Practical Consequences

The overarching theological themes of Scripture should take precedence over and interpret particular texts when there is any divergence between a particular text and a consistent theme of Scripture. Presbyterian theologians, North and South, in the early 1800s justified the social status quo of slavery because there was no particular proof-text that said it was wrong. Today we believe that Jesus' summary of the law, "love God and love your neighbor," negates the practice of slavery. We also agree that Paul's principle enunciated in Galatians 3:28, "There is no longer Jew or Greek, there is no longer slave or free, there is no longer male and female; for all of you are one in Christ Jesus," takes precedence over particular, culturally derived commands for women to be silent.

In the twentieth century we have been led to understand that we have applied God's revelation to us in ways that were often inadequate and sometimes sinful. A missionary friend once helpfully commented that in reading Scripture one needs to take into account not only what God said, but what the people were willing to hear. God, for example, commanded Israel to avoid the idolatry of the Canaanites. Israelite kings sometimes applied that commandment by slaughtering every man, woman, and child in cities they conquered. Are we to believe that is what God intended? No! We need to heed God's warning against idolatry, but we also need to reject the ancient application of genocide. It is important that we untangle the great revelational themes of Scripture from the sometimes misguided concrete cultural applications of them. Interpreting by themes instead of by proof-texts is a good beginning of that process.

Proof-texting is the all too common practice of finding some particular verse of Scripture that, taken out of context, is used to prove something not originally intended. We counter the temptation to seek proof-texts by heeding guideline 4—to be guided by the doctrinal consensus of the church, which is the "rule of faith." The consensus of our creeds and confessions provides us a valuable centering in the themes most common to Scripture. Those common themes are the central principles of the Bible that can provide us a framework within which we reflect on sometimes difficult particular texts.

5. LET ALL INTERPRETATIONS BE IN ACCORD WITH THE "RULE OF LOVE."

The "rule of love" comes from Augustine and can be found in two of our Reformation era Confessions. Its roots lie in Jesus' twofold commandment to love God and to love our neighbor. When we find that someone is interpreting Scripture in a way that is demeaning to God or hurtful to people, we can and should question the validity of that interpretation.

Remember: These seven guidelines are meant to be taken together. If any one were taken separately and applied in isolation, we might develop a one-sided and imbalanced viewpoint. We might, for example, all have different notions of what is the loving thing to do in a certain instance, so this guideline cannot stand alone. As a part of the whole, however, this principle is very helpful.

This is the practical test: By their fruits you shall know them.

a. Confessional Confirmation

The PCUS report in 1983 notes: "No interpretation of Scripture is correct that leads to or supports contempt for any individual or group of persons either within or outside of the church." Further, it states: "Any interpretation of Scripture is wrong that separates or sets in opposition love for God and love for fellow human being."[25]

The Second Helvetic Confession: "We hold that interpretation of the Scripture to be orthodox and genuine which . . . agree[s] with the rule of faith and love, and contributes much to the glory of God and man's salvation."[26]

The Scots Confession: "We dare not receive or admit any interpretation which is contrary to any principal point of our faith, or to any other plain text of Scripture, or to the rule of love."[27]

b. Practical Consequences

When we bear false witness against our neighbor by demeaning someone's character or capabilities, we offend against the rule of love. Presbyterians now recognize that we did this when we were blinded by the biases taught us in our culture and our own sinful desire for superiority over others, and acted accordingly. We need to recognize and rejoice in the full humanity in God's image of those whom we have taken to be somehow inferior to ourselves. Our past attitudes toward African Americans and women offer cases that we need soberly to ponder.

The text of the 1818 Presbyterian General Assembly pronouncement on slavery, which is usually regarded as a brave statement on the evils of slavery, speaks of slaves only in terms of "their ignorance, and their vicious habits generally."[28] This demeaning attitude toward blacks served as an excuse for the church not to act to abolish slavery. More than forty years later, the 1861 statement of the Presbyterian Church in the Confederate States of America justified slavery with these words: "As long as that race, in its comparative degradation co-exists, side by side, with the white, bondage is its normal condition."[29]

These are the proper public statements of official church pronouncements. Amidst the general population, the pervasive social attitude among whites was that blacks were not fully human, had no feelings that could be wounded, and were unable to maintain family relationships in the ways white people did. See, for a moving example, the culturally accurate and widely influential novel by Harriet Beecher Stowe, *Uncle Tom's Cabin or Life Among the Lowly.*[30]

Another example of the official demeaning of a group is evident in the church's attitude toward women. The treatment of women was usually not overtly violent, but women were also denied full humanity by men. Women were not taken seriously by men. The male form of control was to patronize women, generally acknowledging them as limited in their intellectual abilities and their public capacities. The first mention of women in an official General Assembly action came only in 1811, when their voluntary activities were acknowledged: "It has pleased God to excite pious women to combine in association for the purpose of aiding, by their voluntary contribution (to the church). . . . Benevolence is always attractive, but when dressed in female form possesses peculiar charms. . . . We hope the spirit which has animated the worthy women of whom we speak will spread [to] animate other bosoms."[31]

The words of Matthew LaRue Perrine, a Presbyterian seminary professor, reflect the patronizing attitude with which women were treated: "Who will not delight in the sweet and heavenly work of honoring the weaker vessels, and of endeavoring to make them ornamental and useful in the house of God."[32] The concept of ornamental womanhood perhaps derived from a 1692 treatise by a New England Puritan minister, Cotton Mather, who wrote a manual for women entitled *Ornaments for the Daughters of Zion, of the Character and Happiness of a Virtuous Woman.* By "ornaments" Mather meant the essential qualities that should clothe the female character. These qualities should be limited to piety, sobriety, and righteousness in the wedded and maternal state. Moreover, no female should attempt to assume any authority.[33]

In the cases of slavery and the subordination of women, the church has had to reverse itself from stands that excluded persons from the full exercise of their human and ecclesiastical rights. The *practice* of inclusion usually *precedes* development of a *theory* that permits gracious behavior. By that I mean that ministers, in their pastoral practice, tend to treat each individual human case on its own merit. Nonetheless, they often feel the need publicly to maintain a firm stand on the traditional rule because they do not have a rationale for justifying their pastoral practice of exception.

It is wrong to make judgments about the Bible's application in regard to a category of persons with whom we have little or no personal experience and toward whom we may entertain some overt or subtle prejudice. It still happens that persons in power feel free to make judgments—whites regarding blacks, men regarding women—without consulting the people being judged. In order to see the Scriptures in a more whole light, it is essential that we hear the biblical interpretation of the persons who are being excluded or limited by a majority group.[34]

The rule of love, guideline 5, recommends that we remain open to recognize the full humanity and Christian character of those who are different from ourselves.

6. REMEMBER THAT INTERPRETATION OF THE BIBLE REQUIRES EARNEST STUDY.

One task of biblical scholarship is the study and comparison of ancient manuscripts to determine the most authentic text of the Bible. New translations of the Bible prepared by groups of scholars often produce a text that is actually truer to the original than are earlier translations. Biblical translation has gone on so long and is based on such a large number of manuscripts that we can feel very confident of the accuracy of the text in our contemporary Bibles.

Scholars also interpret the influence of the historical and cultural context in which the divine message has come. Experts in ancient languages, cultures, and philosophies continue to help us to understand nuances of thought and practice that we encounter in Scripture. God's message came to real people who lived in particular cultures. Therefore such issues as the mode of dress, ancient legal codes, and attitudes toward family life shaped the manner in which people applied their understanding of God's word. For example, head coverings for women, rules about travel and meal preparation on the Sabbath, and hierarchical patterns of family life that placed men over women and slaves were taken for granted in certain ancient cultures. Scholarship can help us to discern the difference between (1) something that is found in Scripture just because it was an accepted part of the culture and (2) the new and normative message from God. We need to use all of the scholarly resources available to understand the human, linguistic, historical, and cultural contexts in which the divine message has come.

Scripture contains a clear and central saving message. Its surrounding cultural milieu is not always clear, however. About the latter we need to be patient and tolerant with each other. We must work to understand better the context from which the controversial passage has come. And to understand, we must study.

a. Confessional Confirmation

The Westminster Confession of Faith has ten subsections in its Chapter I on Scripture. Subsection 7 says what we know by experience: "All things in Scripture are not alike plain in themselves, nor alike clear unto all."[35] All right. That is the problem. But then comes the answer: "Yet those things which are necessary to be known, believed, and observed, *for salvation*, are so clearly propounded and opened in some place of Scripture or other, that not only the learned, but the unlearned, in a due use of the ordinary means, may attain unto a sufficient understanding of them."[36] The message of salvation is clear! We don't need a Ph.D. to understand it.

Studying for a Ph.D. usually means investigating issues that are not central and not clear. I can use the phrase just quoted above from the Westminster Confession as an example. I did my doctoral dissertation on the doctrine of Scripture in the Westminster Confession of Faith. Therefore, I had to find out what a phrase like "due use of the ordinary means" meant in the mid–seventeenth century in England. It turns out that the

Presbyterian Puritans felt that the "ordinary means" by which someone learned the message of salvation in Jesus Christ was to go to church and listen to the preacher preach for an hour. No one's salvation depends on knowing that fact, but that knowledge does help us to interpret the meaning of that sentence in the Westminster Confession.

What is more important is the notion that only matters having to do with salvation are both essential and clear. In fact, subsection 8 of the Westminster Confession announces that in "controversies of religion" we are to study Greek and Hebrew.[37] Neither raising our voices with each other nor simply saying our prayers will yield positive results when we are dealing with peripheral but perplexing matters in Scripture. Things that are not clear cause controversies. Scholarship can help us to deal with controversial matters, but we need to do our individual and collective homework.

By saying that we require earnest study, especially regarding controversies of religion, we imply that our ideas and/or our behavior could be wrong. The Confessions in fact are clear about their own fallibility. Indeed, the church has revised its Confessions over the years, as I will illustrate in Part 2 of this book.

In the Scots Confession, for example, the Preface states: "We protest that if any man will note in this confession of ours any article or sentence repugnant to God's holy word, that it would please him of his gentleness and for Christian charity's sake to admonish us of the same in writing."[38]

The Westminster Confession states: "All synods and councils since the apostles' times, whether general or particular, may err, and many have erred; therefore they are not to be made the rule of faith or practice, but to be used as a help in both."[39]

The Westminster Divines resisted putting proof-texts to their confession, did not recommend memorizing the Shorter Catechism, and did not intend that the Westminster Standards should be subscribed to as church law.[40] We have done all these things in American Presbyterianism and nonetheless have acted as if we were being faithful to our tradition. Earnest study of the sources of our faith can free us to evaluate the manner in which we have developed our traditions.

b. Practical Consequences

Scholarly study can have practical consequences. For example, we must take care to note the cultural and social differences between the historical time in which a text was written and our time. Cultures are relative and should never be treated as rigid and timeless expressions of God's will.

Anthropologist Walter Goldschmidt, although affirming the relativity of cultures, notes that people are more alike than their cultures are different.[41] We can draw two important conclusions from Goldschmidt's observation: First, the basic themes of the Bible, therefore, are translatable cross-culturally because they are addressed to the basic humanness of all people. Second, not all of the particular cultural applications in the biblical text apply to those of us not living in ancient Near Eastern cultures. Take, for example, the recurring theme in the Old Testament that God's covenant people should be fruitful and multiply and fill the land. The Old Testament heroes of the faith followed that mandate by taking multiple wives, concubines, and slaves to bear children to them. We can understand the original function of the divine mandate without feeling obligated to follow it today. We not only support monogamous marriage, but need to reflect on God's will for us in a world that is arguably overpopulated and in which we, as Americans, use far more of the world's resources than the people of any other country.

At our best, we have made a practice of preserving the function of biblical principles, but not the form, so this idea is not new. For example, greeting one another with a holy kiss was a Pauline command,[42] and Jesus enjoined his disciples to wash one another's feet.[43] We do not continue the original form of those commands. Rather, we preserve the values of loving fellowship and humble service but have abandoned the letter of the deed in both instances.[44] We must always look for the principle that God intended to inculcate, rather than absolutize our fallible, human, culturally bound response.

We would do well to give special attention to biblical instances that defied the cultural assumptions that were dominant in the time in which they were written as well as the assumptions of our own time. For example, Deborah's leadership as a prophet, judge, and warrior violated societal expectations of women's proper role in all three of those instances. Yet God apparently approved of her behavior, and it was good for the people of Israel. Jesus' willingness to talk to a Samaritan woman violated taboos that forbade Jews to talk to Samaritans and men to talk publicly to women, especially women of such bad reputation. Jesus intentionally acted for the good of people even when it caused him to disobey culturally imposed customs.

Earnest study can have important consequences for us. It can help us distinguish between what is central for our salvation and what is part of the peripheral context of the biblical material. It can aid us in discerning what is normative for us in Scripture and what was simply a relative aspect of the culture of the ancient Near East. Scholarship can make us wary of appealing to natural law or what is "natural," for these assumptions often prove to be culturally conditioned rather than intrinsic to human nature. These are all values of guideline 6 that the interpretation of the Bible requires earnest study.

7. SEEK TO INTERPRET A PARTICULAR PASSAGE OF THE BIBLE IN LIGHT OF ALL THE BIBLE.

We are always to interpret the parts by the whole, the complex by the simple, the peripheral by the central. It is called the analogy of faith. This assumes that there is a central unifying theme in Scripture—Creation, Fall, and Redemption in Jesus Christ. Scripture is not just one thing after another. It is a story about a person. It has a saving purpose.

a. Confessional Confirmation

Our Confessions are clear on this principle. The Second Helvetic Confession says: "We hold that interpretation of the Scripture to be orthodox and genuine which is gleaned from the Scriptures themselves . . . and expounded in the light of like and unlike passages and of many and clearer passages."[45]

The Westminster Confession: "The infallible rule of interpretation of Scripture is the Scripture itself; and therefore, when there is a question about the true and full sense of any scripture (which is not manifold, but one), it may be searched and known by other places that speak more clearly."[46]

b. Practical Consequences

This final principle has a most practical application. Unfortunately, our worldview—the largely subconscious set of assumptions about reality and values that we learn from our culture—initially can be the most powerful interpreter of the biblical text. Every culture has a worldview. It provides an overall framework to the working beliefs of a community. We usually do not question assumptions shared by our families, our schoolmates, and our churches. Only when we experience reality from the perspective of another culture or as an outsider do we reexamine our reality. Only when something causes us to feel dissatisfied with our established beliefs do we think to question them.[47] Our worldview can cause us to fixate on certain details in Scripture and miss the larger liberating message.

A historical example of this can be found in the behavior of Robert L. Dabney, the premier theologian in the PCUS from 1865–1892. Dabney accepted without question the common assumptions of his nineteenth-century Southern culture about the inferiority of those who had been slaves. He allowed particular texts that described the practice of slavery in the ancient Near East to obscure the liberating message of the gospel. Dabney argued against the ordination of African Americans in 1867, with these words: "Every hope of the existence of church and state, and of civilization itself, hangs upon our arduous effort to defeat the doctrine of Negro suffrage."[48] And more than twenty years later, in 1888 he wrote that "the radical social theory" that asserts "all men are born free and equal" was an "attack upon God's Word."[49]

We often forget—or never learn—that the most revered leaders of earlier times were captive to a culture that we now reject. Similarly, we do not question our own worldview assumptions unless and until something causes a profound dissonance with them. Even then, we usually will not give them up until we are offered a new paradigm that explains reality more adequately. It is essential that we recognize this tendency and remain open to new understandings of Scripture as we patiently seek to see Scripture as a whole.

CONCLUSION

If we take these seven principles together as clustering around the center of Jesus Christ, we have a wholesome set of guidelines for interpreting the Bible. They simply remind us of what our predecessors in the Reformed tradition, at their best, have practiced for centuries.

Using these guidelines will not automatically or easily answer any controversial questions or resolve difficult or painful issues. If we use them they will, however, assure two things. First, we will more nearly all be talking about the same thing rather than talking past each other. Second, we will be more sure that we are dealing fairly with all of the factors that need to be dealt with in any given situation. These two attitudes would be of great help to us in dealing with what the Westminster Confession calls "controversies of religion."[50]

Part Two

INTERPRETING THE
REFORMED CONFESSIONS

*A Serious and Solemn Protestation
Made by Every Member of the Westminster Assembly
at His First Entry into the Assembly*

*I A.B. do seriously and solemnly protest in the presence of Almighty
God, that in this Assembly whereof I am a member, I will not
maintain anything in matter of doctrine, but what I think in my
conscience to be truth; or in point of discipline, but what I shall
conceive to conduce most to the glory of God, and the good and peace
of his Church.*

—*Journal of the House of Commons*, July 6, 1643[1]

4

How to Interpret
the *Book of Confessions*

WHAT IS A CONFESSION?

In ordinary English, "confession" means an admission that you have done something wrong. To confess in the theological sense, however, means to affirm, declare, or take a stand for what you believe to be true—for what you have done right![1] The earliest Christian confession is "Jesus Christ is Lord" (Phil. 2:11). All Christians are, by definition, people who confess their faith.

A confession can also be a document that expresses and affirms the Christian faith. Usually a confession of faith is an officially adopted statement that articulates a church's understanding of the meaning and implications of the one basic confession of the lordship of Christ.[2] Most Christian bodies have such written statements of faith. Presbyterians, Roman Catholics, Eastern Orthodox, and Lutherans all have official statements. Anglican, Episcopal, and Methodist churches also have documents of slightly lower official status. Even so-called free churches, such as Baptists, that claim to follow only the Bible often have semi-authoritative statements that guide their beliefs and behaviors. I am using the word *confession* in a generic sense. Statements of faith can also be called creeds, symbols, formulas, definitions, declarations of faith, statements of belief, or articles of faith.[3]

THE PROBLEM OF
INTERPRETING THE CONFESSIONS

A number of books have been written that explain the content of the Confessions in our Presbyterian Church (U.S.A.) *Book of Confessions*, but nothing has been written that explains how

to interpret them. This book should be read along with my
earlier book, *Presbyterian Creeds: A Guide to the Book of Confessions*,[4] which deals with each of the Confessions in
its historical context and identifies and focuses on central
themes.[5] Treating themes in the Confessions has been one implicit way of interpreting them.

Edward A. Dowey, Jr., who chaired the committee that prepared the *Book of Confessions*, wrote *A Commentary on the Confession of 1967 and An Introduction to "The Book of Confessions."*[6]
Dowey appended a harmony of the Confessions, listing twenty-
four topics or themes of Reformed theology in one column and
then showing in parallel columns where these topics were found
in each of the Confessions from the sixteenth century to the
Confession of 1967.[7] More recently, German scholar Jan Rohls,
in *Reformed Confessions: Theology from Zurich to Barmen*, has traced
themes found in the principal Continental and British Reformed
Confessions of the sixteenth and seventeenth centuries, and in
the same book Jack Stotts outlines some central themes of twentieth-century Reformed Confessions.[8]

My book *Presbyterian Creeds: A Guide to the Book of Confessions*
uses as an organizing principle the concept of essential tenets
from our ordination vow: "Do you sincerely receive and adopt
the essential tenets of the Reformed Faith as expressed in the
confessions of our church as authentic and reliable expositions
of what Scripture leads us to believe and do, and will you be instructed and led by those confessions as you lead the people of
God?"[9] I then identify ten themes mentioned in the foundational material early in the *Book of Order*, dealing with the
church's Confessions. These ten themes illustrate what some of
those Christian, Protestant, and Reformed essentials are. They
are not the only themes that can be called Reformed, but they
can serve as examples of the constellation of doctrines that are
characteristic of our Reformed and Presbyterian family of faith.

THE *BOOK OF CONFESSIONS*
AND THE *BOOK OF ORDER*

The overlap between the *Book of Confessions* and the *Book of Order* suggests an area where some implicit interpretation of the
Book of Confessions has occurred. Presbyterians have a *Constitu-*

tion composed of these two books. The *Book of Confessions* embodies eleven documents that have been formative for our faith, from the Nicene Creed in the fourth century A.D. to A Brief Statement of Faith—Presbyterian Church (U.S.A.), adopted in 1991. The *Book of Order* contains the form of government by which Presbyterians order our life as a church.

Both of these books are what are called "subordinate standards," which means that they are secondary standards to the Bible. Holy Scripture is our primary standard, and both our confessions of faith and our principles of government are intended to reflect the teachings of Scripture.

The themes, doctrines, or topics listed in the *Book of Order* are stated in very general terms. They identify ideas that comprise part of the confessional consensus of the church. They avoid the kind of specificity that would lead to divisions between denominations, fostering of sectarian splinter groups, or sanctifying the theological conclusions of one school of thought over others. The concern for delving too much into partisan detail is one reason the General Assembly in recent years has been reluctant to label any particular list of doctrines as "essential tenets."[10]

The great confessional themes in the *Book of Order* are presented in such a way that they represent a general consensus among Presbyterians. We begin our discussion of interpreting the *Book of Confessions* by reminding ourselves of some of the overarching themes of Scripture to which they point us.

THE GREAT THEMES
OF THE REFORMED CONFESSIONS

According to the *Book of Order*, Presbyterians share two doctrines with all Christians. These are catholic, or universal, doctrines in the sense that all Christians, whether Eastern Orthodox, Roman Catholic, or a variety of Protestant, hold to them.

The first is the mystery of the Trinity. All Christians believe that there is just one God, but that God exists and is known to us in the three persons of Father, Son, and Holy Spirit.

The second catholic, essential doctrine is the incarnation of the eternal Word of God in Jesus Christ. Christians believe that we are not alone. God came to be with us in the person of Jesus Christ. The Nicene Creed is emphatic that Jesus is truly God and at the same time truly human, a unique event. A relationship to this Triune God through the divine and human person, Jesus Christ, is, for us, salvation. These two universal doctrines are at the heart of our rule of faith.

We are also grateful inheritors of the sixteenth-century renewal of the church known as Protestant Reformation. Our reforming foreparents identified and added two tenets they believed were essential to Christian faith and life but had been omitted from the ancient creeds. The first is the watchword of Luther's reform movement—justification by grace through faith. Protestants insisted that people could have a direct relationship with God on God's gracious terms. We did not need to work our way to heaven, nor could we contribute anything to our salvation. Jesus Christ, in his life, death, and resurrection, has done everything necessary for our reconciliation to God. We have only to accept Christ's unmerited, gracious activity on our behalf.

The second staple belief of sixteenth-century Protestantism was that Scripture, not the pope or the institutional church, is the final authority for salvation and the life of faith. Protestants rejected the notion that they needed a priest to interpret the Christian message to them. All those who could read or hear the gospel message proclaimed from the Bible could know what God wants them to know about loving God and neighbor.

Presbyterians are first of all just Christians. Second, we are Protestants. Finally, we belong to a particular subfamily of Protestants that is called Reformed. "Reformed" was, originally, a geographical designation. It refers to our Protestant Christian ancestors who resided in what we now call Switzerland and who migrated up through Eastern Europe as far as Poland, and up the Rhine River valley into France, a bit of Germany, and the low countries of Belgium and Holland. Finally, this movement crossed the English channel and deeply influenced Scotland, parts of Ireland and Wales, and took root briefly in seventeenth-century England. Names often associated with the Swiss roots of the Reformation are Ulrich Zwingli, Heinrich Bullinger, and John Calvin. John Knox studied with Calvin in Geneva and took the Reformed interpretation of Scripture back to England and Scotland.

Reformed Christians are often reluctant to own that name. Because they want to be ecumenical, they fear that by identifying themselves as Reformed they will contribute to the division of the Christian community. They want simply to be Christians. And they are. However, the circumstances of our predecessors in the faith lent the Presbyterian church a particular perspective on Christian faith and life. The preface to A Brief Statement of Faith—Presbyterian Church (U.S.A.) affirms: "We are convinced that to the Reformed churches a distinctive vision of the catholic faith has been entrusted for the good of the whole church."[11] A Brief Statement of Faith includes the major tenets of the catholic and Protestant faith as well as those characteristic, though not the exclusive possession, of the Reformed churches. The *Book of Order* indicates some of those Reformed themes.

1. First is *the sovereignty of God.* "Central to this tradition is the affirmation of the majesty, holiness, and providence of God who creates, sustains, rules, and redeems the world in the freedom of sovereign righteousness and love."[12] A Brief Statement of Faith prefaces its assertion of the equality of all people with the phrase "In sovereign love God created the world good."[13] Both of those statements emphasize that God's sovereign rule is one of love, not a harsh or arbitrary control. Reformed Christians emphasize the priority, the initiative, the power of God for our good.

2. A corollary of God's sovereignty is *God's election of people* for salvation and service. Election simply means choice. We choose or elect our leaders in a democratic society. God elected or chose us to be members of the community of faith we call the Christian church. Election is a doctrine of comfort for believers. If God has chosen us, then we cannot unchoose ourselves. Even on our worst days, God holds on to us and guides us like a wise and loving parent.

3. As members of the Christian community, we participate in *the covenant life of the church*, ordering ourselves according to the Word of God. God has made a covenant with us that brings us into relationship with God and with each other. A

Brief Statement of Faith points to the mystery of election and covenant saying, "the God of Abraham and Sarah chose a covenant people to bless all families of the earth."[14] And, of most importance for us, "God makes us heirs with Christ of the covenant."[15]

4. Those who are members of this covenant family are called to *a faithful stewardship of God's creation*. We are responsible for each other. We are also responsible for the world we share with others. A Brief Statement of Faith warns that we "threaten death to the planet entrusted to our care."[16] As stewards, charged with responsibility by God, we must show ourselves faithful in caring for the earth and its inhabitants.

5. One reason that we often fail in our stewardship is that we are prone to *the sin of idolatry*. Biblically, only God, the Creator, is worthy of our complete commitment and devotion. Reformed Christians are not much concerned about atheism. Indeed, we don't think there are any genuine atheists. Everyone believes and trusts in something or someone. When we make any created thing our ultimate concern, whether a crude object or a sophisticated idea, whether material wealth or national pride, then we are committing the sin of idolatry.

6. Repenting the sin of idolatry, we are called to seek justice and live in *obedience to the Word of God*. The American theologian H. Richard Niebuhr described various attitudes that Christians could take to the political, social, and religious milieu of which they are a part.[17] Some Christians, he noted, essentially baptize the secular powers and proclaim that Christ is identical with culture. Medieval Catholicism is an example of this, as is, in our time, the desire to reconstitute a mythical Christian America. Other Christians believe that Christ is always against culture. Certain Mennonites refuse even to vote in order not to be caught up in a world in which they feel alien. Reformed Christians, in contrast, characteristically believe that Christ is the transformer of culture. Reformed Christians can never be at ease, either assuming that the culture is Christian or withdrawing from it. We must work to transform human relationships and the structures of society, in accord with the will of the Word of God, Jesus Christ. This means we feel called to work to make society more like what we believe God wants it

to be—more just and loving in every concrete way. Reformed Christians are not utopians, of course. We do not believe that we will bring the kingdom to earth in our lifetime. We are, however, obligated to try.

When Presbyterians state that Scripture is interpreted by the Confessions, we are referring to two things. First, we refer to the fact that the Confessions unanimously direct our attention to Jesus Christ as our Savior and Sovereign. Second, we mean that the Confessions point us to the overarching themes, the doctrines, the major topics that Christians in every age have discovered in Scripture and found essential to their guidance in living the Christian life.

In the two ways mentioned above, the Confessions helpfully interpret Scripture. However, the Confessions themselves need to be correctly interpreted if they are to function correctly as guides to Scripture. The Bible to be interpreted correctly must be understood as a collection of ancient books that reflect Near Eastern culture. Similarly, the Confessions are products of history from the fourth century A.D. to the twentieth century that reflect Euro-American culture.

For most of us in the Presbyterian Church (U.S.A.), that means that we are closer historically and culturally to the authors of the Confessions than we are to the biblical writers of the ancient Near East. Still, there are significant cultural differences between sixteenth- and seventeenth-century Europe and Great Britain and American culture today. We also need especially to hear our Presbyterian colleagues from non-European backgrounds. They can help us to recognize what is a cultural application and what is a biblical theme in a way that those of European descent might not so easily see. Before we examine basic principles for interpreting the Confessions, we need to remind ourselves of their historical and cultural context.

THE HISTORICAL CONTEXT
OF THE CONFESSIONS

To study history is to study the meaning of texts in their original context. The Scots Confession of 1560, for example, says in Chapter XXIV, "The Civil Magistrate": "We hold that any men who conspire to rebel or to overturn the civil powers, as duly established, are not merely enemies to humanity but rebels against God's will."[18] When reading this it is helpful to know that John Knox and four friends wrote that document for the Scottish Parliament a few days after participating in a successful rebellion that drove out the French allies of the Scottish royal family! If our knowledge were only superficial, we could view their statement cynically as a document intended to benefit themselves now that they had consolidated their power. We can, instead, probe more deeply and come to understand their more complex view of the relation between church and state.

If we do that, we learn several things. First, Knox and his allies assumed that the Scottish Parliament, rather than the royal house, was the true representative of the "civil powers." Second, they assumed monarchy to be necessary for good government. Third, they assumed that "the preservation and purification of religion is particularly the duty of kings, princes, rulers, and magistrates."[19] They had not the remotest idea of the separation of church and state. The issue, for them, as they say later in the chapter, was whether the supreme governmental powers were "acting in their own spheres" or whether they had usurped the rights of the people or of God.

This notion that different classes of persons had different and appropriate rights and duties, although different from our view of society and individual responsibility, yields some insights that can guide us today as well. In chapter XIV, "The Works Which Are Counted Good Before God," the Scots Confession declares:

> To honor father, mother, princes, rulers, and superior powers; to love them, to support them, to obey their orders *if they are not contrary to the commands of God, to save the lives of the innocent, to repress tyranny, to defend the oppressed, to keep our bodies clean and holy, to live in soberness and temperance, to deal justly with all men in word and deed, and, finally, to repress any desire to harm our neighbor* [italics mine], are the good works of the second kind, and these are most pleasing and acceptable to God as he has commanded them himself.[20]

A more nuanced understanding of the position of the authors of the Scots Confession, therefore, is: Obey those in power when they are obeying God, but oppose those in power when they are disobedient to God.

It is not easy to be a Presbyterian. Some churches and religious movements assert that one ought always to obey the government, without exception; others distrust the government and say that it ought always to be opposed. For Presbyterians, it is always a judgment call. We are to obey the government if it is doing right, according to our view of God's will. We are to resist the government if it is doing evil and causing harm to people. This nuanced middle view is what forces Presbyterians to spend so much time studying and debating national issues. We are responsible to support the government when it is acting for human good, but to resist tyranny and defend the oppressed.

What we learn from this discussion of the Scots Confession's attitude toward church and state is characteristic for all of our study of the Confessions. The Confessions help us to respond to Jesus Christ in Scripture in what we call the Reformed and Presbyterian way. That way is a particular view of life and relationships that people in our tradition have found very helpful. The Confessions are a central expression of that worldview.

To realize the benefit of studying the Confessions, we must focus our attention on the great themes of the Reformed and Presbyterian way of looking at life. We must not get bogged down or distracted by particular applications of past ways of living and thinking that fit their time in history but are no longer valid for us. That means that we must study the history of the Confessions in order rightly to appreciate and use them.

THE CULTURAL MATRIX OF THE CONFESSIONS

This is also true of our attitude toward culture. There are approximately six thousand different languages and cultures in the world. Each of them enables people to deal with the necessary functions and requirements of life. For example, we all need food, clothing, shelter, and a religion or philosophy that gives meaning to life. But in each culture, the particular kind of food, clothing, and shelter are relative to what is available and what people are taught is good. So, in some cultures the main food staple is rice, in others potatoes, in others bread.

The kind of clothing people wear is relative to the climate and the kinds of coverings that are available. What parts of the body need to be clothed, and when, is taught us by our culture. The meaning of life and how to live a good life is also taught us by our culture.[21]

Everything that human beings create is culture.[22] We are always *in* our culture. We cannot escape it.[23] Our culture teaches us what is true, valuable, and important. We all have a worldview, a generally subconscious, comprehensive perspective on life. We learn our worldview from our culture.

We can be self-critical and change the attitudes taught us by our culture. That usually happens only when we experience some conflict with our culturally derived values.

The Reformed Confessions reflect biblical themes that are often countercultural when measured against the values of our own twentieth-century culture. These biblical themes can be very helpful to us in reflecting on our own Christian life in the present. At the same time, the writers of the Confessions were persons of their own culture and took for granted many applications of the Christian faith that we would not consider biblical or valid for us. We cannot, therefore, literally and uncritically cite attitudes or actions recommended in the Confessions without taking into account the assumptions of their sixteenth- or seventeenth-century culture. In general, we want to look for the overarching themes and be careful to understand the sixteenth- or seventeenth-century cultural context when particular issues do not quite ring true to us.

After I spoke one day about the Confessions to a group of pastors, two of them asked me about a sin forbidden by the Seventh Commandment according to the Westminster Larger Catechism. They, somewhat jokingly, feared that they were guilty of "keeping of stews, and resorting to them."[24] The word "stews" to them suggested "being in a stew," fretting about things, remaining angry. I relieved their minds by telling them that the word "stews" in seventeenth-century England meant "prostitutes." Their concern was about an issue far from the original meaning of the Westminster Divines. It is not always so easy to clarify a misunderstanding by clarifying the difference in the meaning of a word from one historical period to another, but we need to pay attention to the cultural differences between sixteenth- and seventeenth-century Europe and contemporary America. The Confessions can be sources of knowledge that help us understand the values of our Reformed and Presbyterian heritage. To derive those values we must read them carefully with an eye toward their particular history and culture.

5

General Assembly Policies Regarding Interpretation of the Confessions

A WORD ABOUT PRESBYTERIAN POLITY

The two books of our PC(USA) *Constitution*, the *Book of Confessions* and the *Book of Order*, embody our two complementary traditions. Reformed theology, our theological heritage, is contained in the *Book of Confessions*. Presbyterian polity, or government, is contained in our *Book of Order*.

The word *Presbyterian* comes from a Greek word for elder. Presbyterianism is government by elders. We sometimes refer to ministers of Word and Sacrament as "teaching elders" and ordained lay elders as "ruling elders." Actually, both ministers and ordained laypersons do teaching and governing, although the emphasis varies. One of the important principles of Presbyterianism is the parity of the ministry, which means that in all Presbyterian governing bodies there are to be an equal number of voting ministers and lay elders.

The governmental structure of the Presbyterian church in this country was developed at the same time as was the governmental structure of the United States of America. The principles and processes of our civil government and our church government are very similar. Presbyterians have four levels of policy-making governance: session, presbytery, synod, and General Assembly. The session of the local congregation is made up of the called ministers and elected elders of the congregation; there are over 11,000 congregations in the PC(USA). The presbytery is a regional body of churches in a geographic area. The representatives, or commissioners, to the presbytery are an equal number of ministers and lay elders representing all of the

churches. The PC(USA) has 172 presbyteries covering the en-
tire United States. The synod represents a wider geographic area
and encompasses all of the presbyteries in that area; there are
seven synods. Finally, the General Assembly is an annual meeting with some 600 elected commissioners, half ministers and half
lay elders, representing all 172 presbyteries.

You can see that these governing bodies fit together, with each
larger and more inclusive body encompassing the smaller bodies
within it. Authority in the PC(USA) moves both up and down.
Local sessions can, for example, initiate overtures (proposals for
legislative action) that can move up through the presbyteries to
the General Assembly. If approved by the General Assembly,
they move down to affect all the lower governing bodies.

Parallel to these legislative bodies is a rising series of church
courts that deal with disputes regarding the actions of persons
or governing bodies. The presbyteries, the synods, and the
General Assembly each have a Permanent Judicial Commission
(PJC). These courts are composed of persons experienced in
the life of the church and knowledgeable about the *Constitution*.
Often, members of Permanent Judicial Commissions are at-
torneys or judges in their professional lives.

Decisions of lower governing bodies or lower courts may be
appealed to higher courts. For example, any commissioner can
enter a formal complaint against the action of a presbytery that
can then be acted on by the synod PJC. The decision of the
synod court could be appealed to the General Assembly PJC.
The Permanent Judicial Commission of the General Assembly
is like the United States Supreme Court. There can be no appeal from its decisions, which are final. Of course, the General
Assembly could make a new policy that might change the situation in the future.

The purpose of pausing for this review of Presbyterian government is to help you understand the historical examples that
will illustrate the principles in the second part of this book.
Presbyterians like doing things "decently and in order."
Therefore, when we have disagreements about the interpretation of Scripture and the Confessions, they get worked out in
debates in our governing bodies and decisions by our church
courts. Studying the actions of elected representatives in our

governmental system is a concrete way to understand how Presbyterians deal with personal and social problems.[1]

GENERAL ASSEMBLY POLICIES

General Assembly policies also give us some clues as to how contemporary Presbyterians interpret the *Book of Confessions*. The closest analogy would be to the manner in which we interpret the Bible. In Part 1 of this book we examined seven guidelines for interpreting Scripture that were adopted by the UPCUSA General Assembly in 1982. Certainly these guidelines for interpreting Scripture can provide analogies or guidance for interpreting the Confessions. The Confessions are not Scripture, of course, the most obvious difference being that the church sometimes amends or changes its confessions and adds new confessional documents. Scripture is neither amended nor supplemented by additional documents. This basic difference means that there must be some differences in the appropriate method of interpreting the Confessions.

Both the questions posed to church officers at ordination and the foundational material on the Confessions in the *Book of Order* offer some constitutional guidelines for interpreting the Confessions, even though that is not their primary purpose. We therefore turn first to these sources for direction. Then we will review briefly the insights of two other documents that have been adopted by the General Assembly—a 1986 report entitled "The Confessional Nature of the Church" and a 1997 paper entitled "The Assessment of Proposed Amendments to the Book of Confessions." Neither of these documents provides general guidelines for interpreting the *Book of Confessions*, however. The first is directed to questions regarding ordination, and the second applies to the process to be used when a new confession is proposed for inclusion in the *Book of Confessions*. Nonetheless, they give some insights into recent concerns as to how the Confessions are to be interpreted.

The *Book of Order* on the Ordination Vows

After Presbyterians are called to leadership in the church as ministers, elders, or deacons, they are set apart to these offices in a ceremony called ordination. They are asked to give assent to nine vows indicating their commitment to serve Christ through the church. The third of these vows, after the vows regarding trust in Jesus Christ and acceptance of the Scriptures as God's Word, is the vow to be instructed and led by the Confessions:

> Do you sincerely receive and adopt the essential tenets of the Reformed Faith as expressed in the confessions of our church as authentic and reliable expositions of what Scripture leads us to believe and do and will you be instructed and led by those confessions as you lead the people of God?[2]

This ordination vow regarding the Confessions implies several factors regarding the interpretation of the Confessions. First, it implies that the *Book of Confessions* contains both essential and nonessential material. The essential elements must be discerned because only they are to be received and adopted. Second, the phrase "authentic and reliable expositions of what Scripture leads us to believe and do" implies that the Confessions are not exact copies of Scripture but are generally dependable interpretations of the Bible. The final phrase indicates that the primary function of the Confessions is to teach us doctrine and guide us in living the Christian life. The Confessions are not presented as irreformable church law but as a practical help to living the Christian life.

The *Book of Order* on the Confessions

The *Book of Order* indicates the purpose of confessional statements: "The Presbyterian Church states its faith and bears witness to God's grace in Jesus Christ in the creeds and confessions in the Book of Confessions."[3] Pointing to Christ is the primary purpose of the Confessions.

The functions of the Confessions are also articulated in the *Book of Order*:

> They serve to strengthen personal commitment and the life and witness of the community of believers, a people known by conviction as well as by action. They guide the church in its study and interpretation of the Scriptures; they summarize the essence of Christian tradition; they direct the church in maintaining sound doctrines; they equip the church for its work of proclamation.[4]

In laypersons' language, the functions include:

1. Personal growth in conviction by believers;
2. Guidance for the church in the interpretation of the Bible;
3. A summary of the essentials, or main points, of the Christian tradition;
4. Guidance for the church in maintaining theological orthodoxy;
5. Enabling the proclamation of the gospel by directing preachers to its principal themes.

Despite these many and important functions, however, the *Book of Order* goes on to make clear that the confessional statements are subordinate, or secondary, to Jesus Christ and the Scriptures that bear witness to him:

> The confessions are subordinate stands in the church, subject to the authority of Jesus Christ, the Word of God, as the Scriptures bear witness to him. While these standards are subordinate to the Scriptures, they are, nonetheless, standards. They are not lightly drawn up or subscribed to, nor may they be ignored or dismissed. The church is prepared to counsel with or even to discipline one ordained who seriously rejects the faith expressed in them. Moreover, a more exacting amendment process is required to change the *Book of Confessions* than is required to change the remainder of the *Constitution*. Yet the church, in obedience to Jesus Christ, is open to the reform of its standards of doctrine as well as of governance. The church affirms "Ecclesia reformata, semper reformanda," that is, "The church reformed, always being reformed," according to the Word of God and the call of the Spirit.[5]

This lengthy paragraph sets forth the complex relationship that Presbyterians have to their confessional statements. First, they are clearly subordinate, or secondary, sources of guidance. Authority resides with Christ, not with the Confessions in themselves. It is the Bible that bears witness to Christ. The Confessions, in turn, bear witness to their authors' understanding of the Bible.

The Confessions play an important role, nonetheless. They are standards that the church has adopted. It is not enough for church officers merely to acknowledge the existence of the Confessions. They are to function as guidance in the life of office bearers in the church.

The importance of the Confessions is indicated in two ways. An office bearer is subject to counsel or even dismissal by the governing body to which the officer belongs, that is, the session or presbytery, if the officer self-consciously denies the faith expressed in the Confessions. Here the governing body has to discern what essentials of the faith embodied in the Confessions are relevant in a particular situation.

That the Confessions have more gravity than the *Book of Order* itself is illustrated by the fact that it is more difficult to make changes in the *Book of Confessions*. The *Book of Order* can generally be amended by a majority vote in the presbyteries. The process for amending the *Book of Confessions*, however, requires a study committee, a revision committee, the affirmative vote of three consecutive General Assemblies, with the affirmative vote of two-thirds of the presbyteries prior to the last General Assembly vote. Clearly, the Confessions are more central to Presbyterian faith than is church government.

The very human and time-conditioned character of the Confessions is acknowledged by the fact that they can be changed. The church seeks to be open to the continuing call of the Holy Spirit. Therefore, even long-treasured doctrinal views can and must be changed when the church becomes convinced that it has a new and deeper understanding of the Word of God. Significant omissions, reinterpretations, and additions to the doctrinal statements in the *Book of Confessions* have been made during our history as American Presbyterians.

After summarizing the essential content of the *Book of Confessions*, noting ten doctrines or themes of Scripture to which the *Book of Confessions* points us, the *Book of Order*'s discussion of the Confessions concludes with this summary statement: "The creeds and confessions of this church reflect a particular stance within the history of God's people. They are the result of prayer, thought, and experience within a living tradition."[6] Presbyterians would certainly acknowledge that this is not the only legitimate stance that Christians can take, but it is the stance, or attitude, or commitment that is most characteristic of who Presbyterians are. The Confessions are not new, but neither are they antiquated. They are part of a "living tradition." That tradition lives as we actively appropriate it in our lives and ministries.

GUIDELINES ADOPTED
BY THE GENERAL ASSEMBLY

Particular occasions in the life of the church have stimulated the General Assembly to call for study of the application of the Confessions. Anticipating the reunion of the Northern and Southern streams of Presbyterianism in 1983, bodies within both denominations initiated study of the confessional nature of the church, especially as it applied to ordination to church office. The completed study was received by the General Assembly and commended to the church for study in 1986. The report was titled "The Confessional Nature of the Church."[7] Its "guidelines" were adopted by the General Assembly "as guidance for individuals and groups concerned with ordained office in the church."[8]

About a decade later, after several proposals to add documents to the *Book of Confessions* had come before the Assembly, the Assembly asked the Office of Theology and Worship to prepare a paper giving guidance as to how to evaluate such proposals.

In 1997, the General Assembly adopted a report prepared by the Office of Theology and Worship entitled "The Assessment of Proposed Amendments to the Book of Confessions." This report is to be used when the church contemplates changes to the *Book of Confessions*. The document draws on "The Confessional Nature of the Church" and pairs it with discussion of the Confessions in the *Book of Order* as "the church's articulated position."[9] The document's primary new contributions are to suggest two things: (1) When a new confession is proposed for inclusion in the *Book of Confessions*, the church must understand the rationale for its formulation; and (2) The document should be tested in the church for a period of time before taking formal action. These two guidelines are intended to enable the church to discern if the proposed statement is really foundational to the church's faith and life and thus is worthy of adoption.[10]

These two documents can be considered sanctioned and recommended by the General Assembly. They offer a limited sort of "official" interpretation of the *Book of Confessions*, although they themselves need to be interpreted and put into historical context. Each of the papers was adopted by a General Assembly and could be superseded by a subsequent Assembly. They give us some insights into particular concerns for confessional interpretation in the contemporary church. I will draw on these documents as I explain a series of guidelines that I have developed for the interpretation of the Confessions.

6

Guidelines for Interpreting the *Book of Confessions*

This chapter contains seven guidelines for the interpretation of the Confessions. I have based them on my research on how the church has actually used the Confessions. These guidelines are intentionally parallel to the seven General Assembly–approved guidelines for the interpretation of Scripture. I refer to the 1986 report on "The Confessional Nature of the Church" and the 1997 paper "The Assessment of Proposed Amendments to the Book of Confessions."[1] I also include examples from the historical practice of the church in interpreting the *Book of Confessions*. Taken as a whole, these guidelines give a reliable picture of how the church has used the Confessions as a resource in doctrinal and ethical disputes.

In developing these guidelines, I have followed the method of Coach Wooden. That is, I point out how we have done it wrong, and then I show how we have changed and learned to do it right. For each guideline I have chosen an issue that was of central importance in the life of the church, an issue in which the church was struggling to define its life in relation both to Scripture and American culture. These issues are ones in which the change that the church made is clear and unambiguous. I first show how the church misunderstood Scripture and misused the Confessions to support the cultural status quo. Then I show how we changed. Finally, I add statements from current General Assembly policy to show that our new insights have been incorporated into the ongoing life of the church. We observe in each of the issues a common pattern of change that can be instructive for us in dealing with future controversies. We can take hope in observing how the church, under the guidance of the Holy Spirit, has been able to correct its mistakes by gaining new insight into Scripture and reinterpreting, amending, or adding to the Confessions.

Presbyterian church leaders have sought to guide people in faithfulness to Scripture and in harmony with the Confessions. For the most part, history has judged their mistakes to be the result of assumptions held in error by almost everyone in their historical period and cultural context.

I rarely get into trouble for doing something that I know is wrong, because when I know something is wrong I can avoid it. But I sometimes find myself in difficulty because it never occurred to me that my words or actions would create a problem. It is very difficult to be self-critical. My endeavor to examine the way the Confessions have been interpreted in the past is such an effort.

Our foreparents in the faith were sometimes so immersed in their culture that they could not interpret Scripture and the Confessions in ways other than they had been taught. It is especially important to note the power that theories of interpretation had on the way people read and followed Scripture and the Confessions. My criticism is not directed at the people themselves but at the methods of interpretation that proved inadequate. My hope is that we might learn better how to interpret Scripture and the Confessions. My intent is to describe methods of interpretation that will prove adequate to the challenges of our time. The seven proposed guidelines that follow are a concrete step in that direction.

SEVEN GUIDELINES FOR INTERPRETING THE BOOK OF CONFESSIONS

1. THE REDEMPTIVE GOSPEL OF JESUS CHRIST IS THE CENTRAL THEME OF THE *BOOK OF CONFESSIONS*, AS IT IS OF SCRIPTURE.

a. An Example from Presbyterian History: Slavery

A painful but instructive lesson in biblical and confessional interpretation is offered by the manner in which Presbyterians responded to the issue of slavery. In 1787, before there was even a General Assembly, the Synod of New York and Philadelphia took up the matter and established a pattern that lasted into the mid–nineteenth century. In principle, Presbyterians were for liberty, but in practice they tended to minimize the problem inherent in slavery and even viewed slaves as "dangerous." Governing bodies, including the first General Assembly in 1789, counseled that the church take "prudent measures, consistent with the interest and the state of civil society." The commissioners to the General Assembly apparently hoped that by sufficiently educating slaves there might "eventually" be a final abolition of slavery.[2] Presbyterians in this matter were behaving as they perceived good citizens of the new republic should. They were primarily concerned with the well-being of society in general. In practice, they allowed the proliferation of slave holding to go unchecked and its evils to continue largely unexamined.

In 1837 the Presbyterian church split into Old School and New School divisions. The Old School had much of its membership strength in the South and hoped to avoid a split over slavery. The New School, on the other hand, was numerically strong in the Northeast, where abolitionism was strong. In 1845, the year that saw both the Methodists and the Baptists divide over slavery, numerous memorials and petitions were presented to the General Assembly. The General Assembly stated its problem thusly: "The question which is now unhappily agitating and dividing other branches of the Church, and which is pressed upon the attention of the Assembly . . . is, *whether the holding of slaves is, under all circumstances, a heinous sin, calling for the discipline of the Church.*"[3]

The Doctrine of the Spirituality of the Church

The 1845 Assembly responded to the issue first by articulating a new definition of the church. "The Church of Christ is a spiritual body, whose jurisdiction extends only to the religious faith and moral conduct of her members. She cannot legislate where Christ has not legislated, nor make terms of membership which he has not made."[4] This statement, which came to be known as the doctrine of the Spirituality of the Church, mandated a complete separation between church and state such that the church was never to speak on what it believed to be social issues. Southern theologian James Henley Thornwell defined the position in these words: "The silence of Scripture is as real a prohibition as a positive injunction to abstain. Where God has not commanded, the Church has no jurisdiction."[5] Silence was in practice a support for the status quo. It inhibited the Presbyterian church in the South from speaking out against evils in society for seventy years.

In addition to defining the church as a purely spiritual body, the General Assembly articulated a new theory of biblical interpretation, one not used in previous Assembly deliverances. It was the demand for a specific proof-text to warrant any action. The Assembly announced: "It is impossible to answer this question [whether slavery is a sin] in the affirmative without contradicting some of the plainest declarations of the word of God. . . . In so saying, however, the Assembly are not to be understood as denying that there is evil connected with slavery."[6]

The Assembly argued: "The Apostles of Christ sought to ameliorate the condition of slaves, not by denouncing and excommunicating their masters, but by teaching both masters and slaves the glorious doctrines of the gospel, and enjoining upon each the discharge of their relative duties."[7] This statement represented a shift from using general themes of Scripture, such as love of neighbor and the golden rule, as models of behavior. Instead, the rule for interpretation became a demand for explicit proof-texts for specific actions and the assertion that in the absence of a specific condemnation of slavery, it must be allowed.

The primary author of this new approach to the issue of slavery was, not surprisingly, a Southerner, James Henley Thornwell of South Carolina, one of the largest slave-holding states. Thornwell played an important behind-the-scenes role in the definitive statement of the Old School church on slavery in 1845. A commissioner, he wrote to his wife during the Assembly: "I have no doubts but that the Assembly, by a very large majority, will declare slavery not to be sinful, will assert that it is sanctioned by the word of God, that it is purely a civil relation with which the Church, as such, has no right to interfere, and that abolitionism is essentially wicked, disorganizing, and ruinous."[8] Thornwell regarded the abolition of slavery, rather than slavery itself, to be sinful. In 1850, in a famous sermon on slavery, Thornwell contended that the "parties in this conflict are not merely Abolitionists and Slaveholders; they are Atheists, Socialists, Communists, Red Republicans, Jacobins on the one side, and the friends of order and regulated freedom on the other."[9]

What brought about this shift from reading the Bible as the story of God's law of love and Christ's mercy and acceptance, to reading the Bible as a collection of inspired facts that can be organized into a system in accord with contemporary notions of what is reasonable? There is a simple explanation: By the mid–nineteenth century, Presbyterian theologians, including Thornwell, followed Turretin's theology and Scottish Common Sense philosophy. They developed a theory of interpretation that treated the Bible as a book of inerrant facts. Beginning in 1845, slavery was justified on the basis that no particular verse of Scripture explicitly said that it was wrong.

A Biblical Defense of Slavery

The Assembly action of 1845 bought time but could not prevent the inevitable. The Old School Presbyterian church split into Northern and Southern sections in 1861 over the issue of slavery. On December 4, 1861, representatives of forty-seven former Old School Southern presbyteries gathered in Augusta, Georgia, to form the Presbyterian Church in the Confederate States of America. James Henley Thornwell prepared, and the new denomination published, an *Address of the General Assembly of the Presbyterian Church in the Confederate States of America to all the Churches of Jesus Christ Throughout the Earth*. This document remained the definitive statement of how the Bible and the Confessions were to be interpreted in Southern Presbyterianism into the 1930s.

Thornwell's was a sophisticated method of interpretation that clearly specified the hermeneutical rules that were to be used. "Let it be distinctly borne in mind that the only rule of judgment is the written word of God." Thornwell also seems to have viewed the Westminster Confession of Faith as the functional equivalent of Scripture, saying, "Her creed is an authoritative testimony of God, and not a speculation . . . and what she proclaims, she must proclaim with the infallible certitude of faith."[10]

When Thornwell addressed the question: Do the Scriptures *directly* condemn slavery? his answer was, No. "Slavery is no new thing. . . . It has not only existed for ages in the world, but it has existed, under every dispensation of the covenant of grace, in the Church of God. . . . Moses surely made it the subject of express and positive legislation, and the Apostles are equally explicit in inculcating the duties which spring from both sides of the relation. . . . They treat slaves as bound to obey and inculcate obedience as an office of religion."[11]

He then examined another approach. Do the Scriptures indirectly condemn slavery? Again his answer was, No. "The attempt is to show that the genius and spirit of Christianity are opposed to it. Much stress is laid upon the Golden Rule and upon the general denunciations of tyranny and oppression. To all this we reply, that no principle is clearer than that a case positively excepted cannot be included under a general rule."

He concluded, "Let us concede, for a moment, that the laws of love, and the condemnation of tyranny and oppression, seem logically to involve, as a result, the condemnation of slavery; yet, if slavery is afterwards expressly mentioned and treated as a lawful relation, it obviously follows, . . . that slavery is, by necessary implication, excepted."[12]

Thornwell thus articulated a clear interpretive approach that mandated that the presence or absence of proof-texts took precedence over the general principles of the law of God and the gospel of Christ. Theologians such as Charles Hodge at Princeton used this same method of biblical and confessional interpretation, for it fit with the philosophical and cultural assumptions of the early nineteenth century. It seemed that Isaac Newton's laws of physics explained everything about the world and thus that the status quo in society guaranteed order and stability.

b. How the Church Changed Its Mind

Up until the 1930s, Presbyterian seminarians studied Turretin or Turretin's method in the textbooks of Charles Hodge, Thornwell, and Robert Lewis Dabney, Thornwell's successor as the Southern Presbyterian's most influential theologian.[13] But beginning in the 1930s and 1940s a new, christological approach to the interpretation of Scriptures began to take hold. Instead of viewing the Bible as a collection of inerrant facts that Turretin had organized into a system, Presbyterians began to investigate the total ministry of Jesus and listen to his overall message.

In the 1940s, Presbyterian seminarians began to study Calvin and his theology rather than the theology of his interpreters. They also began to study contemporary theologians like Karl Barth, Emil Brunner, and others who treated the Bible with both an attitude of reverence and the use of the tools of current scholarship.[14]

As I noted earlier, in Chapter 2, a new way of interpreting Scripture began to take hold in the 1940s. A theological resurgence began in the 1930s in Europe and reached America with strength in the 1940s. Theologically it centered in Neo-Orthodoxy.[15] In biblical studies it took the form of an amorphous but important "biblical theology movement."[16] Presbyterian scholars led the way. In the South, they included Arnold Rhodes, John Bright, Donald G. Miller, and Balmer H. Kelly.[17] The old debate over reliable authority versus human authorship was bypassed. Instead of viewing the Bible as a collection of inerrant facts, the new theology affirmed that the very human Bible recorded a very real encounter of a real God with real people.[18] Presbyterian scholar Eugene March later wrote: "It seems clear in retrospect that the main concern among Presbyterian biblical theologians of the '40s and '50s was to declare the validity of the Presbyterian premise of biblical authority in such a way as to steer clear of the mistakes of both Liberalism and Fundamentalism."[19] However, it was especially the rationalism of Turretin and Common Sense philosophy that had so dominated Presbyterian theology in the preceding era that needed correction.[20]

Changes in Society and in the Church

Social changes provided the circumstances that mandated that the new biblical and confessional understandings be put into practice. On May 17, 1954, the Supreme Court rendered its decision in *Brown v. Board of Education* that ordered the desegregation of public schools. The Presbyterian Church in the United States (PCUS) was ready. The General Assembly, meeting ten days later on May 27, adopted the recommendations of its Council of Christian Relations "That the General Assembly affirm that enforced segregation of the races is discrimination which is out of harmony with Christian theology and ethics." It then urged that the church at all judicatory levels, from the local session to the General Assembly, be open to people of all races.[21]

The General Assembly further commended the principle of the Supreme Court's decision and urged its members to aid those charged with its implementation.[22] The PCUS was thus the first major church body in the United States to endorse the Supreme Court decision. Most believed that the Assembly would have condemned enforced segregation even if the court had not just spoken.[23]

A Repudiation of Proof-texting and the Spirituality of the Church

In 1956, the clearest ecclesiastical statement to date that rejected the biblical justification of slavery was made in a report that focused on the biblical justification for the equality of women. In its final statement on the principles of biblical interpretation, the committee, which was mandated in 1955, wrote:

> Coming closer to our own day, we no longer argue that human slavery is justified by the Bible, and in accord with God's will. Some of our grandfathers did so argue, declaring that slavery was God's permanent institution. Through the illumination of the Holy Spirit, we have come to a different understanding on this subject. We see that the Bible passages they quoted were not kept by them in the larger context of the Bible as a whole.[24]

This statement countered clearly and directly Thornwell's 1861 argument that the particular text should have priority over the general principle. Now in interpreting the Bible, the Bible was to be seen as a whole in terms of its themes of salvation and service. That meant keeping Christ as the central interpretive principle.

The 1845 doctrine of the Spirituality of the Church was finally and decisively repudiated by the PCUS in the 1960s. Many heroic people—pastors, church officers, students—led the way in supporting full civil and ecclesiastical rights for African Americans. Dr. J. Randolph Taylor and others founded "A Fellowship of Concern" that was very influential in changing attitudes, especially among ministers. Its first principle was "to interpret the Reformed doctrine of the sovereignty of God and the Lordship of Christ in its authentic and historic application to all of life."[25]

The principles and practices of A Fellowship of Concern revealed a profoundly different ecclesiology than that of Thornwell. PCUS ministers now defied the traditional doctrine of the Spirituality of the Church. In 1964, commissioners to the General Assembly voted to amend the Directory for the Worship and Work of the Church to say that "No one shall be excluded from participation in public worship in the Lord's house on the ground or [sic] race, color, or class."[26]

New Confessions with a Christological Focus

The change in biblical interpretation led to new confessional statements that embodied the new method of interpretation. Regarding Scripture, the Confession of 1967 said: "The one sufficient revelation of God is Jesus Christ, the Word of God incarnate, to whom the Holy Spirit bears unique and authoritative witness through the Holy Scriptures, which are received and obeyed as the word of God written."[27] This christological interpretation of Scripture was the basis of a commitment to racial reconciliation in the Confession of 1967. The authors of the Confession of 1967 believed that God's reconciling work in Jesus Christ was the heart of the gospel in any age and that the church of that generation was especially called to the ministry of reconciliation.[28] Regarding race, the Confession of 1967 said: "God has created the people of the earth to be one universal family. In his reconciling love he overcomes barriers between brothers and breaks down every form of discrimination based on racial or ethnic difference, real or imaginary. Therefore the church labors for the abolition of all racial discrimination and ministers to those injured by it."[29]

The new christological hermeneutic had also taken root in the South. The PCUS General Assembly in 1976 adopted "A Declaration of Faith" that said: "When we encounter apparent tensions and conflicts in what Scripture teaches us to believe and do, the final appeal must be to the authority of Christ."[30] On race, the Declaration said: "The antagonisms between races, nations and neighbors . . . are manifestations of our sin against God."[31] The Presbyterian church's silence on the sin of slavery and racial segregation was finally overcome by a christological interpretation of Scripture.

c. General Assembly Policy

General Assembly policy affirms that the Confessions are a compilation not of laws, but of the church's witness to Christ as known in Scripture. The *Book of Order* states: "These confessional statements are subordinate standards in the church, subject to the authority of Jesus Christ, the Word of God, as the Scriptures bear witness to him."[32]

The report on "The Confessional Nature of the Church" affirms: "The Confessions of the Book of Confessions are standards, in response to the historical context of the time, which are subordinate to Scripture; They are subject to criticism in light of the word of God in Jesus Christ as witnessed in the Scriptures of the Old and New Testament and may be revised by the Church following duly prescribed procedures."[33]

Although the Confessions give us an orientation toward Scripture, they are themselves to be interpreted by the perspective of Jesus Christ. The redemptive gospel of Jesus Christ is the central theme of the *Book of Confessions*, as it is of Scripture.

2. THE PLAIN TEXT OF EACH CONFESSION MUST BE INTERPRETED IN ITS OWN HISTORICAL AND CULTURAL CONTEXT TO UNDERSTAND ITS ORIGINAL MEANING.

a. An Example from Presbyterian History: Presbyterian Puritan Customs

Presbyterian Puritans in the seventeenth century were reformers. They were loyal members and ministers of the

Church of England. They wanted to reform the church from within in a more Calvinistic direction theologically and a more Presbyterian direction governmentally. In a time of Royal absolutism in the state, they were voices for democracy. In a time of defense of the status quo in the church, they argued to change practices that had long been sacrosanct. They were determined to remove all remnants of "popery," such as the wearing of elaborate vestments in worship. These Presbyterian Puritans were, however, also people of their own time and culture. The manner in which they applied their understanding of the gospel would, in many instances, be inappropriate, indeed impossible, today.

Marriage and Puritanism

The Westminster Confession laid down a principle regarding marriage: "It is lawful for all sorts of people to marry, who are able with judgment to give their consent. Yet, is it the duty of Christians to marry onely in the Lord."[34] The anti–Roman Catholic bias of seventeenth-century English Puritanism was such that the principle was applied in this manner: "And therefore such as profess the true reformed Religion, should not marry with infidels, papists or other idolaters." In fact, in the original edition of the Westminster Confession, the pope was branded the Anti-Christ![35]

Seventeenth-century English Puritanism also reacted to the celibacy required of the Roman Catholic priesthood, so for Puritans marriage was virtually required. Indeed, "undue delay of marriage" is specified as a sin in the Westminster Larger Catechism.[36] In sixteenth- and seventeenth-century Protestantism, marriages were still often arranged by the parents. The Second Helvetic Confession mandates: "Let marriages be made with consent of the parents, or of those who take the place of parents."[37] Marriage was very much a public concern, not something to be left to the discretion of the persons involved, and it usually took place at what we would consider a very young age. Even for Reformers and Puritans, the primary purpose of marriage was the propagation of children.

Personal Behavior and Puritanism

Contemporary American Presbyterians are not like seventeenth-century Puritans in our personal behavior. We no longer keep a Puritan sabbath. The Westminster Catechisms enjoin us from "profaning the day by idleness, or doing that which is in itself sinful, or by unnecessary thoughts, words, or works, about our worldly employments or recreations."[38] That eliminates anyone from engaging in any recreation or thinking about his or her weekday work on Sunday.

We all engage in what the Puritans thought were "worldly amusements." They categorized as sinful "lascivious songs, books, pictures, dancings, stageplays, and all other provocations to, or acts of, uncleanness either in ourselves or others."[39] It would be difficult to watch television without violating Puritan standards.

We all dress in ways that the Puritans (and our grandparents) would have thought "immodest apparel."[40] Anyone who wears a bathing suit to the beach would be sinning by seventeenth-century Puritan standards.

Puritan Attitudes toward Worship

Of more importance, some of our worship practices violate Puritan standards. Most of our churches display religious art, which was forbidden in seventeenth-century Puritan England. The Westminster Larger Catechism designates as sin "the making of any representation of God, of all, or of any of the three Persons, either inwardly in our mind, or outwardly in any kind of image or likeness of any creature whatsoever."[41] Thus, every Sunday School room that displays a print of Sallman's "Head of Christ" is sinful by the standards of the Larger Catechism.

In another example, some of our "charismatic" members are engaging in sin by Puritan standards. The Confessions demand: "Therefore, let all strange tongues keep silence in gatherings for worship, and let all things be set forth in a common language which is understood by the people gathered in that place."[42] "Prayer . . . is to be made . . . if vocal, in a known tongue."[43]

It would simply not be possible today to apply literally some of the injunctions of the Confessions. Nor should we. The task for Christians is to fulfill the spirit of Christ's gospel in ways appropriate to our own time and culture.

b. How the Church Changed Its Mind

The Confessions can give us guidance by showing how Presbyterian Christians applied their understanding of the faith in their time and culture. We must, however, creatively apply the gospel in our own time and culture. The common thread between the seventeenth century and today is the biblical values and commitments that we share. Across time and culture we affirm, for example, honesty in our business dealings, fidelity in personal relationships, loyalty to the Christian community, and ultimate trust in Christ alone. It is when we move beyond these and other general values to applying them in a particular cultural setting that conflicts may appear.

Changes in Presbyterian Attitudes toward Marriage with Roman Catholics

American Presbyterians, beginning in 1930, reacted against the ban on marrying Roman Catholics, recognizing that "many Roman Catholics are sincere and intelligent believers in our Lord Jesus Christ."[44] Presbyterians later amended the Westminster Confession of Faith to remove the offending statements against the pope[45] and marriage with Roman Catholics.[46]

Our task is not, therefore, to attempt to replicate the cultural forms of the sixteenth or seventeenth century regarding marriage. Rather, we should seek to apply the functional values of marrying "in the Lord" in ways that are appropriate in our time and culture.

Moving beyond Puritan Behaviors in the Confessions

The church must endeavor to apply the intended biblical and confessional function, but not the culturally limited and limiting form of past ideas and practices. After understanding the original meaning in context, we can attempt to discern what is applicable to our time and situation. We can take our guidance from the architectural principle that form should follow function. One should first decide the purpose, or function, of the projected building and *then* determine the style of building that will be best suited. The same principle is true in interpreting Scripture and the Confessions.

One of the best illustrations of the application of this principle in biblical and confessional interpretation is found in a 1956 PCUS report on the status of women. The committee developed certain considerations based on the denomination's confessional stance. They were convinced that a solution could be found in accord with the Westminster Confession of Faith principle that "The infallible rule of interpretation of Scripture is the Scripture itself; and therefore, when there is a question about the true and full sense of any Scripture (which is not manifold, but one), it may be searched and known by other places that speak more clearly."[47]

The committee applied this principle, saying: "We find it clearly and unmistakably stated in Scripture that God endowed at least some women for leadership among His people in Bible days. Therefore, we conclude that what God has done, and has promised to do (Acts 2:17) may be done in our own day."[48]

In this instance, Presbyterians in the 1950s went beyond the Puritan customs of the 1640s and found a principle in the Confessions that enabled them to apply the gospel in a liberating way. The Confessions reflect the culture of the sixteenth and seventeenth centuries regarding the role of women and the purpose of marriage. The Confessions also embody principles of freedom and equality that we can apply in ways they were prevented by their culture from applying. Under the leadership of the Spirit of Christ, we can find values in Scripture and the Confessions that will allow us to do new things that go beyond the historical and cultural limits of the Confessions.

c. General Assembly Policy

Our church has recognized this principle and acknowledged it in our *Book of Order*: "Thus, the creeds and confessions of this church reflect a particular stance within the history of God's people."[49] The report on "The Confessional Nature of the Church" commented:

Confessions have a *provisional authority* (and are therefore subject to revision and correction) because all confessions are the work of limited, fallible, sinful human beings and churches. In our time we have perhaps become more aware than most of those who wrote and adopted Reformed confessions in the past that even when confessions intend to serve only the revealed truth and will of God, they are also influenced by the sexual, racial, and economic biases and the scientific and cultural limitations of a particular situation.[50]

Taking seriously the plain text of the Confessions does not mean reading them with a surface literalism. Rather, the plain text of each confession must be interpreted in its own historical and cultural context to understand its original meaning. Then, under the leading of the Spirit of Christ, we can discern what is applicable to us today.

3. THE HOLY SPIRIT LEADS US TO CLEARER AND MORE COMPLETE UNDERSTANDINGS OF THE TRUTH OF SCRIPTURE AND THUS OF THE *BOOK OF CONFESSIONS*.

a. An Example from Presbyterian History: The Role of Confessions

In the late nineteenth and early twentieth centuries, Presbyterian professors treated the Westminster Confession of Faith as the functional equivalent of Scripture. Dr. W. M. McPheeters, a professor at Columbia Seminary from 1888–1932, for example, contended that no teacher in any of the seminaries had any right to teach anything contrary to the Scriptures, the Westminster Confession of Faith, or the traditional interpretations of the Confession. The denomination as a whole shared that attitude. Partly in reaction to confessional changes proposed in the North, in 1894 the PCUS even attempted to ensure that no changes would be made in the confessional standards by changing the requirement that two-thirds of the presbyteries must approve a change in the Confessions to require a three-fourths vote in the presbyteries to effect change.[51]

Between 1888 and 1893 there were unsuccessful attempts in the Northern PCUSA denomination to amend the Westminster Confession of Faith. The issue behind the attempts was the strong emphasis in the Westminster Confession on God's sovereignty and God's election of persons to salvation. Dr. Henry Van Dyke, a professor at Princeton and a proponent of revision, stated the issue: "These two truths, God's *sovereignty* in the bestowal of his grace, and his *infinite love for all men*, are the hinges and turning points of all Christian theology. The *anti*-Calvinist decries the first. The *hyper*-Calvinist or Supralapsarian decries the second, holding that God creates some men on purpose to damn them, for his glory. . . . The ultimate and dominant reason why I advocate the revision of the Westminster Confession is that it does not state these two truths in their relations and harmony."[52]

The attitude toward the Confession itself was a deciding factor in the defeat of revision. Ironically, persons with opposite views of the value of the Westminster Confession united in opposing its revision. Van Dyke characterized the situation: "The extreme conservative wants to keep the Confession just as it is, because he thinks it is as near perfection as any thing human can be. He has no hope of bettering it. The extreme radical wants to keep it unchanged, because *he* thinks that is the surest way to lay the whole thing on the shelf, and cause it to be regarded simply as a grand old historic monument of what that eminent body, the Westminster Assembly of Divines, believed."[53]

In 1900, the PCUS had a great debate over whether to place a footnote in the Westminster Confession indicating that children dying in infancy would be saved. Leading PCUS theologians protested any change to the Confession, even to adding an explanatory note, on the ground that the Westminster Confession explicitly said what Scripture said and no more or less.[54]

b. How the Church Changed Its Mind

Additions to the Westminster Confession of Faith

In 1903 in the Northern stream, the PCUSA General Assembly added to the Westminster Confession of Faith a Declaratory Statement and two additional chapters, "Of the Holy Spirit," and "Of the Love of God and Missions." The additions were meant to correct misunderstandings of the doctrine of election and to remedy omissions in the Confession regarding the love of God and missions.

The Declaratory Statement is an instance of an official interpretation of the Westminster Confession written to correct misunderstandings of the Confessions. For example, the Statement says: "*First*, With reference to Chapter III of the Confession of Faith: that concerning those who are saved in Christ, the doctrine of God's eternal decree is held in harmony with the doctrine of his love to all mankind. . . . That concerning those who perish, the doctrine of God's eternal decree is held in harmony with the doctrine that God desires not the death of any sinner."[55] The Declaratory Statement continues: "*Second*, With reference to Chapter X, Section 3, of the Confession of Faith, that it is not to be regarded as teaching that any who die in infancy are lost."[56]

The additions were proposed by a committee that included former President Benjamin Harrison and Associate Justice of the Supreme Court John Harlan, a member of the New York Avenue Presbyterian Church in Washington, D.C. The proposed additions were designed to respond to two issues that had not been prominent in the thinking of the Westminster Divines. First, Christian experience, manifested in revivals, was a significant feature of American Presbyterian life and necessitated a statement on the Holy Spirit. Second, the worldwide missionary movement that began in the nineteenth and twentieth centuries seemed to Presbyterians to warrant a statement on the love of God for the whole world. Clearly, a new attitude prevailed that no longer identified the statements in the original form of the Westminster Confession with a comprehensive and complete exposition of Scripture.[57]

At the same time, Henry Van Dyke wrote, and the church adopted, a "Brief Statement of the Reformed Faith." Its sixteen short articles were written in a devotional tone and unified by the theme of love. Although the statement did not have confessional authority, it interpreted and modified the more rigid aspects of the seventeenth-century Westminster Confession for many people.[58]

In 1942, the Southern stream of Presbyterianism, the PCUS, amended the Westminster Confession of Faith by the addition of two chapters, "Of the Holy Spirit" and "Of the Gospel." The form and the effect of these added chapters were very similar to the chapters adopted by the PCUSA in 1903.[59]

A Changed Interpretation of the Westminster Standards

In the 1940s, both the attitude toward the Confession and its interpretation changed. In 1940, E. T. Thompson, professor at Union Theological Seminary, was attacked in the church press for failing to maintain a traditional interpretation of the faith. His accuser was a Charlotte, North Carolina, businessman, Tom Glasgow. Glasgow assumed that the historic position of the Presbyterian church was the same as that of B. B. Warfield, an Old Princeton professor who had died in 1921. Regarding the inspiration of the Bible, Glasgow argued from the Old Princeton position that the Bible was "an oracular Book, as the Word of God, in such a sense that whatever it says, God says."[60]

E. T. Thompson's synod supported him. Thompson requested that his presbytery examine him, however, because Glasgow, by refusing to press formal charges, gave Thompson no opportunity to defend himself. The presbytery exonerated Thompson. Its judgment was precedent setting, because it specifically denied that a theological professor was bound to accept the interpretation placed upon the Confessions by his predecessors.[61]

In 1961, the PCUS General Assembly forthrightly admitted that a certain statement of the Westminster Confession of Faith was biblically unsound: "That the General Assembly declare that in its judgment the doctrine of fore-ordination to everlasting death as formulated in the [Westminster] Confession is not an adequate statement of the Christian faith." The Assembly argued that the doctrine "as stated in the Confession is not essential to Reformed theology," noting "its absence in this vigorous form in such authentic Reformed creeds as the Scots Confession of 1560, the Second Helvetic Confession, and the Heidelberg Confession." The Assembly emphasized the importance of "studying the Confession in the context of

the *total* Reformed tradition."[62] Thus, the church has reinterpreted, amended, and added to the *Book of Confessions* and will
continue to do so.

c. General Assembly Policy

General Assembly policies confirm both that the Confessions
are standards to be taken seriously and that they are not exact
replicas of the Scriptures. Regarding the need to take the Confessions seriously, the *Book of Order* states: "Moreover, a more
exacting amendment process is required to change the confessions of the church than is required to change the Constitution
in matters of government, discipline, or service."[63] Requiring
two-thirds of the presbyteries to affirm a change in the Confessions shows the seriousness with which Presbyterians take
their historic doctrinal formulations. The report on "The Confessional Nature of the Church" links the two issues: "The
Confessions of the Book of Confessions are standards, in response to the historical context of the time, which are subordinate to Scripture; . . . and may be revised by the Church
following duly prescribed procedures."[64]

Regarding the idea that the Confessions do not duplicate
Scripture, the report on "The Confessional Nature of the
Church" indicates a practical implication of the human, historical, and cultural conditioning of the Confessions. It states:
"When individuals or groups in the church call into question
some aspect of the confessions or of the church's interpretation
of them, those who hear that objection should consider the
possibility that the dispute may point to a deficiency in present
confessional standards, remembering that, indeed, synods or
councils may err and that the church is always to be reformed
(semper reformanda)."[65]

If the Presbyterian church had never changed its interpretation of the Bible and its doctrinal standards, it would not
have been able to cope with new situations. The worldwide
missionary movement, for example, would never have begun.
The Holy Spirit, as Jesus promised, leads us to clearer and
more complete understandings of the truth of the Bible; thus
we are better able to understand the central teachings of the
Book of Confessions.

4. OVERARCHING THEMES THAT RUN THROUGH THE *BOOK OF CONFESSIONS*, FROM THE ANCIENT CREEDS TO THE MOST CONTEMPORARY STATEMENT OF FAITH, ARE THE RULE OF FAITH.

a. An Example from Presbyterian History: Essentials of Belief

The Adopting Act of 1729

The great themes of the *Book of Confessions* are those essential elements of faith that link us to other believers as Christian, Protestant, and Reformed believers. The concept of essential tenets of belief is rooted in the Adopting Act of 1729, the earliest attempt to define the Confessions as a rule of faith. It set the pattern for all subsequent efforts of Presbyterians to understand their Confessions as a rule of faith.

In 1729, as the church attempted to define in what sense the Confessions were a rule of faith, the debate was over whether ordinands had to subscribe to the Westminster Confession of Faith and Catechisms. On the one side, Jonathan Dickinson, pastor in Elizabethtown, New Jersey, spoke for those who believed that all authority for faith and life came from Christ as revealed in Scripture.[66] Dickinson said: "I have a higher opinion of the Assembly's Confession than of any other book of the kind existent in the world, yet I don't think it perfect. I know it to be the dictates of fallible men, and I know of no law, either of religion or reason, that obliges me to subscribe to it."[67] He argued for erring, if at all, on the side of being inclusive: "We may not so much as shut out of Communion, any such Dissenters, as we can charitably hope Christ won't shut out of heaven."[68]

Representing the other side was John Thomson, a pastor in the Presbytery of New Castle, who wanted strict subscription to the Westminster Standards. He asked: "Now a church without a confession, what is it like?" For him it was like "a city without walls." He then argued: "For if we have no confession which is ours by synodical act, or if any among us have not subscribed or acknowledged the confession, . . . there is no bar provided to keep out of the ministry those who are corrupt in doctrinals."[69]

The Adopting Act was a classical Presbyterian compromise. It decreed that Yes, every minister did have to subscribe to the Westminster Confession; however, only in its essential and necessary articles. If the minister had a "scruple," or difference of opinion, with the Confession, the Presbytery would decide whether the article in dispute was essential. Finally, the Adopting Act exhorted all to civility toward those with whom they disagreed on nonessentials.[70]

The Fundamentalist/Modernist Controversy

In times of uncertainty in American society and in the church, the attitude of compromise in the Adopting Act has been severely tested. The common worldview that most American Christians shared was upset by two events in the mid–nineteenth century. The first was the Civil War which forced Americans to realize that all Christians did not interpret the Bible alike and did not share the same deep values on the crucial issue of slavery. The second disruption to the shared worldview was Darwin's theory of evolution. People were forced to choose between the older worldview that assumed divine order, design, and unchanging reality, and the new outlook that was agnostic and assumed natural selection and constant change.[71] Persons who clung to the older worldview and resisted Darwinism and modern trends became known as Fundamentalists.[72] Those who adopted a modern scientific worldview and sought to synthesize the Christian faith with modern knowledge were called Liberals or Modernists.[73]

By the end of the nineteenth century, America was in transition from a rural to an industrial economy. In the church, new methods of studying the Bible challenged the assumptions of its literary inerrancy. In 1881 the term "higher criticism" was introduced to describe a method of studying the forms and sources of the biblical texts with the tools of scientific and literary criticism. This was different and more threatening to Fundamentalists than "lower criticism," which dealt with establishing the best text from a study of ancient manuscripts.[74] Fundamentalists resisted higher criticism as a liberal threat.

What became known as the Fundamentalist/Modernist controversy in America began as a conflict between Charles Augustus Briggs, a professor of Old Testament at Union Seminary in New York, and Benjamin Breckenridge Warfield, Professor of Didactic and Polemical Theology at Princeton Theological Seminary. Briggs supported higher criticism, believing that evangelical Christians should not allow the new scholarship to be monopolized by the extreme liberals. Warfield rejected higher criticism and supported biblical inerrancy. Briggs also supported the movement that eventually led to the modifications of the Westminster Confession in 1903 (see Guideline 3, Section b). Warfield opposed any revision of the Confession. Briggs, as the librarian at Union, had spent his summers in bookstores in England purchasing and reading the writings of the Westminster Divines. He accused Warfield and the Princeton faculty of teaching Turretin and Scottish Common Sense instead of the theology of the Westminster Confession. Warfield and his colleagues insisted that their theology *was* that of Westminster.[75]

Briggs and Warfield conducted a literary debate in the pages of *The Presbyterian Review*, of which they were co-editors. The debate ceased and the church conflict began when Brigg was inaugurated at Union in 1891 in the newly created chair of Biblical Theology and gave his address on the authority of Holy Scripture. In it he characterized the Princeton theory of inerrancy and resistance to biblical criticism as the principal hindrances to the true functioning of biblical authority.[76] The General Assembly of 1891 received overtures from sixty-three presbyteries concerning Briggs' address.

In 1892, the General Assembly in Portland issued a Deliverance that "Our Church holds that the inspired Word as it came from God is without error." The Presbytery of New York was instructed to try Briggs on the charge of heresy for denying the inerrancy of the Bible. Chairman Birch of the prosecuting committee for the New York Presbytery exemplified the attitude of the extreme conservatives who were pushing the case when he said of the Bible: "God is the arranger of its clauses, the chooser of its terms, and the speller of its words so that the text in its letters, words, or clauses is just as divine as the thought."[77]

Briggs affirmed his belief in Scripture as the only infallible rule of faith and practice and was acquitted of all charges by the presbytery. The prosecution appealed to the General Assembly. In 1893, the General Assembly sustained the appeal and recommended that Briggs be suspended from the Presbyterian ministry and that Union Seminary, because it had declined to dismiss Briggs, no longer be considered a Presbyterian seminary. Eight-seven commissioners protested the statement of the Assembly that the inerrancy of the Bible was taught in the Westminster Confession of Faith, saying that this was "an interpretation of our standards which they never have borne."[78]

Five Essential and Necessary Doctrines

The conflict that had erupted in the Briggs case continued in the new century. In 1910, the General Assembly adopted a five-point declaration of "essential and necessary doctrines" that all candidates for ordination had to affirm.

The Bills and Overtures Committee of the Assembly recommended a doctrinal Deliverance prefaced by their perspective on the societal situation:

> It is an age of doubt. Many elements of the faith delivered, once for all, to the saints, and embodied in the immemorial testimony of the Christian Church, are by many openly questioned and rejected. Thereby the fundamentals not only of our faith as a Church, but of evangelical Christianity, are assaulted. Laxity in matters of moral opinion has been followed by laxity in matters of moral obligation. It is an age of impatience, of no restraint. The spirit of license and lawlessness is abroad.[79]

The committee then appealed to the Adopting Act of 1729, noting that if a candidate had "scruples" about articles "not essential and necessary in doctrine," he should "declare his sentiments to the Presbytery or Synod," which then would be called upon to decide what was essential and necessary. The committee, however, proposed that the General Assembly not wait for a candidate or a case, but, prior to any particular case, should make "a declaration with regard to certain essential and necessary articles of faith."[80]

The committee recommended and the Assembly adopted five points as "certain essential and necessary articles of faith." The five points were: (1) the inerrancy of the Bible; (2) the virgin birth of Christ; (3) Christ's death as a sacrifice to satisfy divine justice and reconcile us to God; (4) Christ's bodily resurrection; and (5) the authenticity of Christ's mighty miracles that made changes in the order of nature. Each was preceded with the phrase "It is an essential doctrine of the Word of God and our Standards, that . . ." The section concluded with the statement: "These five articles of faith are essential and necessary. Others are equally so. We need not fear for God's truth as it is revealed in the Holy Scriptures and contained in our Westminster Standards."[81]

The Five Points became a creed within a creed, functionally supplanting the Westminster Confession. The five "essential and necessary doctrines" were reaffirmed by General Assemblies in 1916 and 1923. By the 1920s, the Five Points, with some changes, became known as the Five Fundamentals and provided a rallying point for conservative Christians across denominational lines.[82]

In 1923, J. Gresham Machen, now the leader of the conservative party at Princeton Seminary, published a book entitled *Christianity and Liberalism*. In it he declared that liberalism was "un-Christian" and a different religion from Christianity. Machen asserted: "A separation between the two parties in the Church is the crying need of the hour."[83]

The Auburn Affirmation

One year later, in 1924, thirteen percent of the ministers in the Presbyterian Church (U.S.A.) signed the Auburn Affirmation. This statement argued that the Five Points, or essential and necessary doctrines, that the Assembly had reaffirmed the previous year were theories that went beyond the facts of Scripture to which the Westminster Confession of Faith obligated them.[84] The majority of the more than twelve hundred ministers who signed the Auburn Affirmation were pastors of large churches.[85]

In the second and third sentences of the Affirmation, the signers made clear their acceptance of Westminster:

At the outset we affirm and declare our acceptance of the Westminster Confession of Faith, as we did at our ordinations, "as containing the system of doctrine taught in the Holy Scriptures." We sincerely hold and earnestly preach the doctrines of evangelical Christianity, in agreement with the historic testimony of the Presbyterian Church in the United States of America, of which we are loyal ministers.[86]

However, in response to the Doctrinal Deliverance of the 1923 General Assembly, the signers declared:

Some of us regard the particular theories contained in the deliverance of the General Assembly of 1923 as satisfactory explanations of these facts and doctrines. But we are united in believing that these are not the only theories allowed by the Scriptures and our standards as explanations of these facts and doctrines of our religion, and that all who hold to these facts and doctrines, whatever theories they may employ to explain them, are worthy of all confidence and fellowship.[87]

Causes of Unrest in the Denomination

By 1925, there were three identifiable parties within the Presbyterian church—liberals, fundamentalists, and moderates. The theological liberals believed in an inclusive church that welcomed everyone who wanted to belong. At the opposite extreme were the exclusivists, doctrinal fundamentalists who argued for an exclusive church composed only of those who would affirm the five essential and necessary articles they had developed. The largest group, though less well defined, were the moderates who were theologically conservative but accepted inclusivism for the peace, unity, and mission of the church. This middle group contained both signers of the Auburn Affirmation and adherents of the Five Points who deplored the controversy.

In 1925, the General Assembly elected as Moderator Professor Charles R. Erdman of Princeton, a moderate who had been working for reconciliation. During the Assembly the exclusivists pushed through a measure to allow the General Assembly to review the ordination of ministerial candidates suspected of not affirming the Five Points. Henry Sloan Coffin, a liberal, speaking for the Presbytery of New York, declared the Assembly's action unconstitutional and announced that the presbytery would not abide by it. The stage was set for a denominational split. Moderator Erdman left the chair and proposed a Special Theological Commission "to study the present spiritual condition of our Church and the causes making for unrest, and to report to the next General Assembly, to the end that the purity, peace and unity and progress of the Church may be assured."[88] Both Coffin and former Presidential candidate William Jennings Bryan, an exclusivist leader, seconded the motion.[89]

b. How the Church Changed Its Mind
An Interim Report: Tolerance

That same summer of 1925, William Jennings Bryan became the object of national attention during the Scopes trial in Dayton, Tennessee. Bryan prosecuted Scopes for teaching evolution in the public schools. Although Bryan won the case, the first trial to be heard nationally on the radio, public opinion turned against his militant style of defending the literal interpretation of the Bible.[90]

The following spring, in May of 1926, the Special Theological Commission presented an interim report. Enumerating many causes of unrest in the church, it focused on the necessary balance of common faith and toleration:

> Foremost among the forces making for unity is a common faith expressed in our confessional symbols, but intimately related to this, and defining the way in which the faith is to be held among brethren in the Presbyterian Church, is the constitutional principle of toleration.[91]

Later in the report it declared:

> The principle of toleration when rightly conceived and frankly and fairly applied is as truly a part of our constitution as are any of the doctrines stated in that instrument. . . . Presbyterianism is a great body of belief, but it is more than a belief; it is also a tradition, a controlling sentiment. The ties which bind us to it are not of the mind only; they are ties of the heart as well.[92]

The Final Report: What the General Assembly Cannot Do

The final report of the Special Theological Commission, in 1927, took up the question "What authority, if any, does the General Assembly possess for declaring any article to be an essential and necessary one in a sense which renders its statement mandatory and applicable to all cases."[93] The report first noted that according to the Adopting Act of 1729, the decision as to essential and necessary articles was to be made only in regard to specific cases. Second, it noted, the authority was to be exercised by the governing body directly involved in the ordaining of ministers. (In that day, the General Synod also functioned like a presbytery.) Third, nothing in the Act of 1729 is inconsistent with "the principle that the Presbytery's right to determine the fitness of the candidate is paramount."[94]

The report then struggled mightily to understand the meaning of the phrase "essential and necessary." It concluded that the term "essential" referred, in the language then used for ordination, to the "system of doctrine taught in the Holy Scriptures." Interestingly, the report in 1927 concluded that "these distinctions are too close and scholastic for the practical purpose contemplated by the question now before us."[95] (Since that time the Presbyterian church has abandoned the language of "system of doctrine" with reference to Scripture, for we recognize that the Scripture is not a system, and so to characterize it thusly is to distort its character.)

The conclusions of the report have had major implications for Presbyterian belief and behavior up to the present time. The report decided that the General Assembly did not have the authority to decide "as a general proposition, that certain articles, when considered abstractly and logically, are essential and necessary to the system of doctrine contained in the Holy Scriptures." The report concluded that "to declare broadly that an article is essential and necessary, it would be required to quote the exact language of the article as it appears in the Confession of Faith. It could not paraphrase the language nor use other terms than those employed within the Constitution, much less could it erect into essential and necessary articles doctrines which are only derived as inferences from the statements of the Confession."[96]

What We Can Learn from These Controversies

The Adopting Act was a model Presbyterian compromise. It attempted to balance confessional standards for the community with freedom of individual conscience. The Act distinguished between essentials and nonessentials in the confessional standards and allowed the governing body affected to make the judgment as to which doctrines were essential. It asked for civility in the treatment of members of the governing body, even when they disagreed over what the body deemed as nonessentials.

The General Assembly of 1910, while appealing to the Adopting Act, upset the balance. Instead of allowing an individual to present a matter of conscience to a governing body, the General Assembly acted unilaterally to make a preemptive judgment. Instead of distinguishing carefully between essential and nonessential elements in theology, the 1910 Assembly and its successors in 1916 and 1923 declared the theories explaining the great facts of salvation to be as essential as the biblical facts themselves.

For example, one of the central affirmations of Protestant Christianity is the authority of Scripture. The first of the Five Points, however, is a theory, inerrancy, that attempts to explain the manner in which the Bible's authority is manifested. Similarly, Point 3, Christ's sacrificial death to satisfy divine justice, is only one of many different biblical images that seek to explain how it is that Christ's death for our sins is effective for our salvation. By insisting on certain theories as the only correct explanation for some of the great doctrines of the faith, the Fundamentalists lifted nonessential points of theology to the level of essentials of the faith. The result was to disrupt the unity of the church.

Do Presbyterians believe that there are essential tenets of the faith in the *Book of Confessions*? Yes! It would make no sense to ask deacons, elders, and ministers to "sincerely receive and adopt the essential tenets" if there were none. Why, then, do some Presbyterians prefer that we not speak of essential tenets? The answer lies in the disrupting effect of the Fundamentalist/Modernist controversy, which most Presbyterians do not want to repeat. The solution to this problem lies in our understanding of that history.

What we have learned in this brief examination of our history is that "essential tenets" properly refers to the great overarching principles of our faith such as those mentioned in the *Book of Order:* the mystery of the Trinity; the Incarnation of the eternal Word of God in Jesus Christ; justification by grace alone through faith; Scripture as the final authority for salvation and the life of faith; God's sovereignty; God's election of people for salvation and service; the covenant life of the church, ordering itself according to the Word of God; a faithful stewardship of God's creation; the sin of idolatry; and seeking justice and living in obedience to the Word of God.[97]

This list of doctrines is not meant to be an exhaustive or exclusive list. It is meant to illustrate the appropriate location and level of our commitment to doctrines in the *Book of Confessions.* The essentials are those great doctrines on which the church as a community agrees.

We agree, for example, that we are called to be stewards of God's creation. That is an essential tenet of the Reformed faith. But we may not bind the consciences of our fellow Presbyterians regarding specific theories, inferences, implications, or applications of the doctrine of stewardship. The committee that worked five years to draft A Brief Statement of Faith—Presbyterian Church (U.S.A.) expressed concern about our stewardship by saying that we "threaten death to the planet entrusted to our care."[98] Despite the deep feelings of many on the committee, it refrained from making confessional a more explicit warning against, for example, nuclear armaments, global warming, or other environmental threats. The committee was conscious of writing a contemporary creed meant to evidence what we believed in common. That contemporary statement, adopted in 1991, bears an unintentional but close resemblance to the group of doctrines set forth in the *Book of Order.* The concurrence of those two parts of our *Constitution* strengthens our understanding of essentials as doctrines stated in their most general form.

The wisdom of the 1927 decision lay in the affirmation that not even the General Assembly should declare as essential specific theories, implications, or applications of the most general doctrines. Consideration of more detailed doctrinal issues should be left to the lower governing bodies, where a particular case can be studied in its context to make the most informed judgment of the relationship between essentials to which the whole community is obligated and nonessentials that should be left to the individual's freedom of conscience.

The rule of faith acts like ripples in a pond, spreading outward from a central point. Jesus Christ is the center point as the one in whom we meet the triune God. Surrounding those universal Christian essential beliefs are the Protestant watchwords *justification* and *scripture*. Yet farther out but encircling these are the characteristically Reformed concepts of sovereignty, election, covenant, stewardship, sin, and obedience. There are many further ripples and rings as we attempt to understand the whole counsel of God. We are most sure that we are dealing with essentials as we move toward the center of the circle. As we deal with doctrinal matters, we are to exhibit civility and tolerance toward one another. That is all part of what we mean by the rule of faith.

c. General Assembly Policy

The importance of keeping our attention fixed on the center of the circle rather than on matters on the periphery explains why Presbyterian ordination vows use the concept of "essential tenets."[99] Presbyterians are not expected to "receive and adopt" every interpretation of Scripture, nor every jot and tittle of all of the centuries of development of the *Book of Confessions*. Instead, we need to stay fixed on the essentials, the center of the Christian, Protestant, and Reformed faith.

With this understanding we affirm the statements in the *Book of Order*: "They [the confessions] guide the church in its study and interpretation of the Scriptures; they summarize the essence of the Christian tradition; they direct the church in maintaining sound doctrines; they equip the church for its work of proclamation."[100]

We can affirm both common confessional standards for the community and freedom of individual conscience. We can embrace both conviction and civility when we understand that the overarching themes that run through the *Book of Confessions*, from the ancient creeds to the most contemporary statement of faith, are the rule of faith.

5. THE CHURCH, AS A RULE OF LOVE, HAS REJECTED, AND SHOULD CONTINUE TO REJECT, CULTURAL NORMS THAT HAVE BEEN USED TO OPPRESS PEOPLE IN THE NAME OF CONFESSIONAL CONFORMITY.

a. An Example from Presbyterian History: The Role of Women

Charles Hodge and Ornamental Womanhood

The Presbyterian church rejects biblical and confessional justifications of the subordination of women. Our historical memory tends to be selective, however, and we easily block out unpleasant attitudes that prevailed in our Presbyterian past.

Charles Hodge was the premier theologian of the Northern Presbyterian stream in the nineteenth century. He was on the faculty of Princeton Seminary for fifty-eight years.[101] He trained three thousand seminarians, more than any other American in the nineteenth century.[102] His annual critical reviews of the General Assembly exercised great influence on future directions in the denomination. His three-volume *Systematic Theology*, published in 1872, remained the standard text at Princeton and in many American seminaries into the 1930s and was used in some as late as 1960.

Hodge, in company with most learned gentlemen of this day, opposed both abolitionism and women's suffrage.[103] "An association of gentlemen," as Hodge and his friends referred to themselves, published the journal *Biblical Repertory and Princeton Review*. Between the years 1825 and 1855 they wrote numerous articles on "ornamental womanhood," a phrase meant to convey the virtues that should characterize a Christian woman.[104] Women, Hodge felt, should express their piety in private. The public realm was for men only.

Hodge, in a negative review of a book that attacked slavery, used the analogy of the necessary subordination of women. He wrote: "If women are to be emancipated from subjection to the law which God has imposed upon them . . . [i]f in studied insult to the authority of God, we are to renounce, in the marriage contract, all claim to obedience, . . . there is no deformity of human character from which we turn with deeper loathing than from a woman forgetful of her nature and clamorous for the vocations and rights of men."[105]

The Kenyon Case Debate

Similar attitudes, though they may have been expressed more gently, persisted into the late twentieth century. Despite the fact that the UPCUSA began ordaining women in 1956, the biblical validity of that ordination was challenged in a celebrated case in the early 1970s involving Walter Wynn Kenyon, a senior at Pittsburgh Seminary.

Kenyon applied for ordination to Pittsburgh Presbytery in 1974. He was part of a group of students who were staunch followers of Professor John H. Gerstner, Jr., who taught a form of Calvinism that was an extension of the Old Princeton theology of Charles Hodge and B. B. Warfield. One of the convictions of this group was that the Bible "clearly teaches women should be subordinate ('silent') in the official teaching and ruling ministry of the Christian Church."[106] Kenyon made clear to the Candidates and Credentials Committee that he believed that the Bible forbade the ordination of women.

Gerstner's followers, including Kenyon, contended that the matter of women's ordination was a nonessential detail of the Presbyterian system of doctrine and governance. Therefore they felt free, in the language of the Adopting Act of 1729, to "scruple" against this point and yet be ministers in good standing in the denomination.

The Candidates and Credentials Committee of Pittsburgh Presbytery recommended against ordaining Kenyon. The committee said he could not affirmatively answer question five (of the eight) ordination questions: "Do you endorse our Church's government, and will you honor its discipline? Will you be a friend among your comrades in ministry, working with them, subject to the ordering of God's word and Spirit?"[107]

The presbytery overruled its committee and recommended ordination for Kenyon. That decision was appealed. The synod reversed the presbytery. The synod's ruling was then appealed to the Permanent Judicial Commission of the General Assembly, which ruled for the synod and against the presbytery and Kenyon.

Kenyon, Gerstner, and several colleagues wrote a pamphlet explaining and defending their position:

> Our purpose is simply to demonstrate what we believe to be the real issue: Biblical authority. . . . The Scriptures consistently teach that in the church and in the home women are placed in a subordinate position. No one can read the Bible and not see authority "writ large" therein. Everywhere we meet a chain of command. . . . Everyone who loves and fears God should acknowledge that the Word of God authoritatively establishes authority—male authority—in the church.[108]

b. How the Church Changed Its Mind

The Kenyon Case Decision

Jack Martin Maxwell, who filed the initial protest against Pittsburgh Presbytery's action to ordain Kenyon believed that the issue was one of polity, because the *Book of Order* already permitted the ordination of women.[109] A careful reading of the decision of the Permanent Judicial Commission (PJC) in 1974, shows, rather, that its decision was based on a theological interpretation of the Confessions.

The PJC argued that the equality of women and men is an essential of Presbyterian theological beliefs, stating: "The question of the importance of our belief in the equality of all people before God is thus essential to the disposition of this case. It is evident from our Church's confessional standards that the Church believes the Spirit of God has led us into new understandings of this equality before God."[110]

The commission's decision affirming the equality of women and men in church leadership was built on the insight of the Confession of 1967 concerning the equality of persons of all races. The PJC cited the Confession of 1967: "Congregations, individuals, or groups of Christians who exclude, dominate, or patronize their fellowmen, however subtly, resist the Spirit of God and bring contempt on the faith which they profess."[111] Following that citation, the commission declared: "The UP-CUSA, in obedience to Jesus Christ, under the authority of Scripture (and guided by its confessions) has now developed its understanding of the equality of all people (both male and female) before God."[112]

No better statement of the confessional principle of the rule of love could be made. It was initially articulated with regard to racial equality and was rightly applied in this case to the equality of women and men.[113] The Permanent Judicial Commission decision illustrated the Presbyterian process of making theological decisions based on the Confessions. The doctrinal principle that runs through the Confessions is the equality of all persons before God. When the church failed to apply that principle to African Americans and to women, it was debated and adjudicated in particular cases until a theological consensus was achieved that the principle did indeed apply to all people.

Confessional Confirmation of the Equality of Women and Men

A definitive confessional statement regarding the role of women was developed in the 1990s. The 1983 reunion of the PCUS and the UPCUSA that formed the PC(USA) ultimately produced a new confession of faith that spoke positively of the role of women in the church. The Articles of Agreement that governed the reunion mandated that the reuniting Assembly instruct its Moderator to appoint a committee "representing diversities of points of view and groups within the reunited Church to prepare a Brief Statement of the Reformed Faith for possible inclusion in *The Book of Confessions*."[114]

It was the first time in the history of Reformed creedal formation that a group was chosen specifically for its diversity and then expected to write a document evoking unity. It was certainly the first time that a significant number of women were engaged in preparing a Reformed confessional document.

For the first time in Reformed creedal history, women were declared equal to men and called to all of the ministries of the church. In lines 29–32, A Brief Statement of Faith announces the equality of all persons: "In sovereign love God created the world good and makes everyone equally in God's image, male and female, of every race and people, to live as one community."[115]

The Confession of 1967 had affirmed the equality of all races. Because of continuing racial discrimination, that confessional commitment was reasserted with vigor in A Brief Statement of Faith. A Brief Statement of Faith, for the first time confessionally, applied the equality of persons specifically to women.

This confessional affirmation was necessary in order to correct the historically limited perspectives of the Scots Confession and the Second Helvetic Confession, both of which teach that baptism should not be administered by women. The context for both confessions was an extremely polemical sentiment against the Roman Catholic practice that allowed nuns and midwives to baptize if it was feared that a child might die unbaptized and thus go to hell. The Protestant Reformers rejected this view and practice. Their manner of stating it was to say that women were not permitted ecclesiastical functions, such as preaching and baptizing.[116]

The women seminary professors on the Brief Statement of Faith Committee noted that contemporary male seminarians often cited these earlier statements in the *Book of Confessions* to argue that women seminarians did not have a valid call to ministry. These women felt that it was necessary, thirty-five years after the decision to ordain women to the ministry, to have a specific confessional warrant for ordination.[117] The final line inserted into the original draft of A Brief Statement of Faith gave that confessional warrant to the ordination of women. Line 64 states that the Spirit "calls women and men to all the ministries of the Church."[118] This immediately follows statements on baptism and the Lord's Supper.

Also, for the first time in a Reformed confession, A Brief Statement of Faith uses feminine as well as masculine language to refer to God: "Loving us still, God makes us heirs with Christ of the covenant. Like a mother who will not forsake her nursing child, like a father who runs to welcome the prodigal home, God is faithful still."[119] The statements comparing God to a mother and a father are taken directly from the biblical text; Mother is from Isaiah 49:15–16, and Father is from Luke 15:11–32.

This use of metaphorical language also militates against a naive literalism in the treatment of biblical language. The authors of A Brief Statement of Faith were clear that God is neither male nor female. They recognized that we use human illustrations to point to the reality of a personal God whose love exceeds that of our best human examples.[120]

c. General Assembly Policy

The Presbyterian church appealed to a twentieth-century confession as it confronted and rejected nineteenth-century cultural norms that continued to oppress women. The action to affirm the equality of women and men informs and gives a greater depth of meaning to the statement in the *Book of Order*: "The Presbyterian Church (U.S.A.) states its faith and bears witness to God's grace in Jesus Christ in the creeds and confessions in the Book of Confessions. In these confessional statements the church declares to its members and to the world who and what it is, what it believes, [and] what it resolves to do. These statements identify the church as a community of people known by its convictions as well as by its actions."[121]

The 1986 report on the Confessional Nature of the Church muses on this process, commenting: "So long as presbyteries do not contradict specific interpretations of the confessions made by the General Assembly, and so long as sessions do not contradict those made by the Assembly and their presbytery, presbyteries and sessions have the right and responsibility to interpret for themselves whether candidates for ordination and ordained persons, for whom they are responsible, hold to the "essentials" of the faith as articulated by the confessions of the church (the constitutional right of appeal being understood)."[122]

Presbyterianism always attempts to balance the rights of the individual and the lower governing bodies with the need for national constitutional norms to which all must adhere. The case of the oppression of women in the name of religion clarifies the fact that governing bodies can err. In this case, the error was corrected by interpreting and applying other confessional writings that had been used to combat other forms of oppression. New confessional statements may be needed in the future to clarify new interpretations of Scripture and the confessional tradition. Both interpretations of past confessions and new confessional affirmations can serve the church in rejecting cultural norms that have been used to oppress people in the name of confessional conformity.

6. THE CHURCH NEEDS TO DO CAREFUL STUDY TO DISTINGUISH BETWEEN THE APPROPRIATE THEOLOGICAL APPLICATION AND THE CULTURAL CONTEXT OF CONFESSIONAL STATEMENTS.

a. An Example from Presbyterian History: A Class System

Historic cultural forms should not be absolutized. Presbyterians have long ignored many of the centrally important sins mentioned in the *Book of Confessions* because we intuitively recognized that they were conditioned by an earlier public, political culture. The sixteenth- and seventeenth-century confessions assume monarchy, a rigid class system, a patriarchal family, and an economic system quite different from our own. Nonetheless, long into our American history, Presbyterians sometimes justified an unjust status quo on the assumption that it was approved in the Bible and the Confessions.

The Assumption of a Class System Based on Race

The Westminster Larger Catechism assumes a rigid class system, specifying in detail class-based sins: "The sins of inferiors against their superiors are . . ."[123]; "The sins of superiors are . . ."[124]; "The sins of equals are . . ."[125] The American revolution was in part about the removal of such class distinctions. Such assumptions of class distinctions in seventeenth-century English society, although assumed in the Westminster Confession, were largely ignored by American Presbyterians.

But class distinctions did exist, and one of the great tragedies of early America was the assumption of a different kind of class distinction—between white and black persons. The peculiarly American blending of the theological rationalism of Turretin, which interpreted the Bible literally, and Scottish Common Sense philosophy, which allowed the assumptions of popular culture to be treated as normative, prevented theologians from recognizing and rejecting this equation of race with class. Historian Mark Noll has declared: "On slavery, exegetes stood for a commonsense reading of the Bible. On race, exegetes forsook the Bible and relied on common sense."[126] Especially in the American South, a literal reading of the Bible as justifying slavery was combined with the cultural assumption that Africans, and only Africans, as a class, were fit and destined for slavery.

Southern theologian James Henley Thornwell, in his 1861 address on behalf of the new Confederate Presbyterian denomination, stated that man's "most solemn earthly interests [are] his country and his race."[127] He went on to assume a class system as natural, biblical, and essential, and argued: "If men had drawn their conclusions upon this subject [slavery] only from the Bible, it would no more have entered into any human head to denounce slavery as sin, than to denounce monarchy, aristocracy or poverty."[128]

Thornwell then subtly shifted the argument from the Bible to the assumption of what was natural according to his white, nineteenth-century perspective, writing: "Whatever is universal is natural. We are willing that slavery should be tried by this standard."[129] Thornwell, as a white Southerner, assumed that human beings should be divided into classes by race: "The truth is, the education of the human race for liberty and virtue, is a vast Providential scheme, and God assigns to every man, by a wise and holy decree, the precise place he is to occupy in the great moral school of humanity. The scholars are distributed into classes, according to their competency and progress."[130] Thornwell said of the slave: "There are no doubt, many rights which belong to other men . . . to his master, for example— which are denied to him. But is he fit to possess them?"[131] The African belonged to a different class than the white man, according to Thornwell's commonsense reasonings: "As long as that race, in its comparative degradation, coexists, side by side, with the white, bondage is its normal condition."[132]

Charles Hodge, the leading Northern Old School theologian, argued that the conditions of slavery should be ameliorated. He believed that treating slaves with the dignity owed to all people under God would eventually lead to the elimination of slavery. Nonetheless, when Hodge reflected on his own nineteenth-century American culture, he could not rid himself of the prevailing assumption that Africans belonged to a lower class. In 1835, he wrote that the traditional "organization of society" was enough to justify making "the free colored man" at birth "a disfranchised outcast." For Hodge it was a truth "on all hands admitted" that blacks "could not, consistently with the public welfare, be entrusted with the exercise of political power." Thus, for Hodge, it was "the acknowledged right of the State to govern them [blacks, slave or free] by laws in the formation of which they have no voice."[133] For Hodge, black people were a separate class.

George Bourne: The Book and Slavery Irreconcilable

A special example of the disaster that accompanied the assumption of a race/class system was provided by the case of George Bourne. In 1815, a Presbyterian minister named George Bourne brought the moral issue of slavery before the courts of the Presbyterian church. While preparing for ordination in 1811, he had noticed that Question 142 of the Westminster Larger Catechism designated "man-stealing" as a sin forbidden in the Eighth Commandment. Bourne further noticed that a footnote to the catechism defined "man-stealing" as slavery.[134]

In 1815, Bourne, who was then Stated Clerk of his presbytery, was a commissioner to the General Assembly for the third time. He presented a paper to the Assembly "in which he asked what should be done with a Presbyterian minister who had taken a Negro slave into his orchard on a Sabbath morning, tied her to an apple tree, stripped off her clothing, lashed her unmercifully until he had exhausted himself, left her tied up, mounted his horse, rode to his meeting house, preached, returned home, repeated the lashing until he had again exhausted himself, called in another man to continue the whipping, rubbed salt in the wounds, and finally released her."[135]

Bourne then proposed an overture to the General Assembly (which he had to present as a commissioner's resolution) that called slaveholding a sin and asked what to do when other Christians refused to commune with slaveholders. He also supported a question from the Synod of Ohio asking whether slaveholders should be excommunicated.[136] The General Assembly, over the next three years, responded to Bourne in several ways. First, in 1816, the General Assembly removed the footnote on "man-stealing" from the Catechism. (The answer to Question 142 in the Westminster Larger Catechism remained, but was ignored.)[137] That same year, 1816, George Bourne published a book entitled *The Book and Slavery Irreconcilable*,[138] in which he discussed the issue of the Bible and slavery.

Second, in 1818, the General Assembly deposed Bourne from the ministry for having brought "reproach on the character of the Virginia Clergy" because he would neither name particular guilty parties nor drop his charges.[139]

Third, also in 1818, the General Assembly made a brave statement against slavery as inconsistent with the law of God (to love neighbor) and the gospel of Christ. However, the statement expressed great sympathy for Presbyterian slaveholders who, it held, were not responsible for this evil and noted that slaves were vicious and could not be immediately emancipated. It hoped for eventual emancipation when it was good for the public welfare.[140]

From 1819 until 1845, overtures regarding slavery were repeatedly presented to the General Assembly. The Presbyterian General Assembly employed two strategies to deal with these repeated overtures. The first was to urge congregations to support the efforts of the American Colonization Society to send freed slaves back to Africa. These efforts had little practical effect on the slavery problem, but provided a means whereby church members could feel that they were doing something about it.[141] The second strategy was simply to refuse to discuss the matter. The Assembly annually laid antislavery motions on the table, and in 1836 the Assembly stated: "Resolved, That this whole subject be indefinitely postponed."[142]

b. How the Church Changed Its Mind
Rejecting the Race/Class System of Slavery

There were exceptions to the dominant Presbyterian pattern of dealing with slavery, and some smaller Presbyterian denominations acted more decisively. In 1811, for example, The Associate Synod (a party to the union in 1858 that formed the United Presbyterian Church in North America) made this declaration: "That it is a moral evil to hold Negroes or their children in perpetual slavery; or to claim the right of buying and selling, or bequeathing them as transferable property."[143] Twenty years later, in 1831, when it seemed that the synod's wishes were still not being acted on, it excommunicated all slaveholders.[144]

Contemporary Confessional Rejection of a Class System

Our twentieth-century Presbyterian Confessions stress the equality of all persons. The Confession of 1967 focuses on reconciliation, denouncing racial discrimination and "enslaving poverty in a world of abundance."[145] A Brief Statement of Faith (1991) plainly contradicts the assumption of a necessary class system, saying: "In sovereign love God created the world good and makes everyone equally in God's image, male and female, of every race and people, to live as one community."[146]

c. General Assembly Policy

The *Book of Order* states: "Yet the church, in obedience to Jesus Christ, is open to the reform of its standards of doctrine as well as of governance. The church affirms 'Ecclesia reformata, semper reformanda,' that is, 'The church reformed, always reforming,' according to the Word of God and the call of the Spirit."[147] Being reformed has meant, among many other things, being willing to reject a class system that does violence to the equality of all persons made in the image of God. Presbyterians have learned that it is wrong to treat people as a class rather than as individuals. Our historical experience warns us of the danger of making culturally accepted assumptions about what is natural and then investing those assumptions with biblical and confessional sanction.

Presbyterians have continued to be reforming by carefully distinguishing between the appropriate theological application and the cultural context of their confessional statements. When necessary, Presbyterians have reinterpreted their biblical and confessional tradition and produced new and more centrally biblical confessions of faith.

7. A STUDY OF THE WHOLE *BOOK OF CONFESSIONS* IS AN INSTRUCTIVE RESOURCE FOR PRESBYTERIANS.

A Review of the Confessions on Human Sexuality

The Confessions can enable us to view reality from the perspective of our parents in the faith who sought to be Christian, Protestant, and Reformed. Following an issue through the Confessions can provide an illuminating study of how those in the Reformed family of faith have wrestled with issues and developed in their understanding of them.[148]

The Presbyterian Church (U.S.A.), along with most American denominations, has been preoccupied with questions regarding sexual relations during the past several decades. A review of how our predecessors have dealt with this in the past can serve as an example of the benefit of using the whole *Book of Confessions* when confronting an issue.

The Nicene Creed and the Apostles' Creed provide brief summaries of the essentials of the Christian faith. Other Confessions in the *Book of Confessions* regard these two creeds, especially the Apostles' Creed, as the foundation on which our confession of faith rests. The Heidelberg Catechism refers to the Apostles' Creed as "our universally acknowledged Confession of faith."[149] The Second Helvetic Confession says, "In short, we receive the Apostles' Creed because it delivers to us the true faith."[150] The Westminster Shorter Catechism concludes by citing the text of the Apostles' Creed.[151]

Neither the Nicene Creed nor the Apostles' Creed mentions sexual relations. It would appear, therefore, that this is not an essential element of Christian faith. It is certainly not a matter that is related to our salvation. Our newest confessional statement, A Brief Statement of Faith, presented a contemporary creedal summary of the Christian faith, but it does not mention sexual relations either.

The Scots Confession does not mention marriage or sexual relations. The Heidelberg Catechism, in its characteristic manner, helps us to think more deeply about the implications of a seemingly simple subject. Commenting on the Seventh Commandment that forbids adultery, Heidelberg says that we should "live chaste and disciplined lives, whether in holy wedlock or in single life."[152]

The Second Helvetic Confession, interestingly, begins with a concern for single people. It speaks of those "who have the gift of celibacy from heaven," but notes that "if the gift be taken away," they should feel free to marry. This Swiss Confession speaks at length about marriage and condemns both polygamy and those who condemn second marriages.[153] The Confession reflects the practical, pastoral approach of Heinrich Bullinger, its author, who recommended that matrimonial courts be established in the church "before whom matrimonial disputes may be settled."[154]

The Westminster Confession (1647), in company with most generally accepted seventeenth-century thought, viewed marriage and divorce as a public issue involving the good of society. According to Westminster, the needs and wishes of the persons involved were to be subordinated to concern for the stability of society, "Wherein, a public and orderly course of proceeding is to be observed: And the Persons concerned in it, not left to their own wills and discretion, in their own case."[155]

The Westminster Confession set a pattern for all subsequent Presbyterian dealing with marriage and divorce by establishing a norm for the community but allowing exceptions for individuals. It outlawed divorce, for that was the norm, but it allowed exceptions for the innocent party in cases of adultery or desertion.

The Westminster Larger Catechism, prepared as a guide for Puritan preaching, made extensive and detailed comments on the Seventh Commandment. In chronicling the sins forbidden in the prohibition of adultery, it broadened the list to include "all unclean imaginations, thoughts, purposes, and affections."[156] In listing the duties required by the Seventh Commandment, it included "conjugal love and cohabitation."[157]

The Barmen Declaration (1934) focused on the need to obey Christ as the Word of God rather than secular powers and ignored the issue of sexual relations. So did the original draft of the Confession of 1967, which focused on three global problems: racial discrimination; enslaving poverty in a world of abundance; and the need for peace, justice, and freedom among nations.[158] The revision committee added a fourth issue—anarchy in sexual relationships.[159] It spoke about human beings' "perennial confusion about the meaning of sex" and stressed that this confusion "has been aggravated in our day"; it then cited, among others, seemingly opposite pressures such as "new means of birth control" and "world overpopulation."[160]

Changes in Science and Society

Scientific developments often lead to changes in society. In turn, the church must enable people to cope with these changes. Characteristic of the church's struggle to come to clarity on such an issue as sexuality was its attitude toward artificial methods of birth control. In 1931, a committee of the Federal Council of Churches recommended that parents consider using artificial means of birth control. The PCUS, in indignation, withdrew from the council. The PCUSA remained a member but asked the council to "hold its peace on questions of delicacy and morality." Thirty years later, in 1960, both denominations adopted a joint statement approving of birth control.[161]

In those intervening three decades, the Presbyterian church had clarified its attitude about the primary purpose of marriage. Into the 1930s, the denomination emphasized the public good and saw the primary purposes of marriage as bearing children, creating a family, and supporting stability in society.[162] By 1960, Presbyterians had adopted the posture that the primary purpose of marriage was personal fulfillment. It was for the mutual comfort, encouragement, and upbuilding of the persons involved; therefore birth control could be accepted. This shift in understanding the purpose of marriage also enabled a more nuanced attitude toward divorce.

a. An Example from Presbyterian History: Divorce and Remarriage

Attitudes toward Divorce and Remarriage

Beginning in 1926, both the PCUSA and the PCUS reflected the ambivalence of both church members and ministers by alternately attempting to rigidify church law by prohibiting any divorce but then expanding the exception clauses that allowed for divorce and remarriage. In 1928, in separate actions, the PCUSA and PCUS attempted to remove "desertion" as a ground for divorce and remarriage. In both cases, the presbyteries turned it down.[163] In 1950, the PCUSA attempted to tighten the definitions of what constituted "satisfactory evidence," "innocent party," and "scriptural grounds," in order to give the presbytery greater control over the whole matter of the remarriage of divorced persons. Ministers and elders voted to reject these moves as "impractical and too mandatory."[164] In 1956, the PCUS sent to its presbyteries an overture that removed all exceptions and recommended no divorce or remarriage for any reason. This was supported on scholarly grounds by an appendix that asserted that the words "except for unchastity" in Matthew 19:9 were not part of the original text and "that these words form no part of Jesus' teaching."[165] The presbyteries voted down this attempt to remove all exceptions to the prohibition on divorce and remarriage.[166]

b. How the Church Changed Its Mind

During a period of about thirty years, the Presbyterian churches were cautiously feeling their way toward a new understanding of the meaning of marriage. They were also endeavoring to apply the new understanding of a christological interpretation of Scripture that began to take hold in the late 1930s.

Sometimes a new hermeneutic can be developed by reaching back to past precedents of biblical and confessional interpretation. A fascinating and little known case is very illuminating for the changes in Presbyterian attitudes toward divorce and remarriage. Even though the Westminster Confession of Faith was not changed until the 1950s, the theological thinking necessary for that change had long been available.

A Theological Precedent

An early exception to the general opposition to divorce in Presbyterianism arose in the matter of slave marriages in the pre–Civil War South.[167] White society did not recognize the validity of slave marriages. Slaves who were husband and wife could be separated and sold, perhaps never to see each other again. Yet slaves had their own rituals for recognizing marriage, and gradually the churches recognized these rituals, despite their informal nature. Presbyterians were among the first to do so.[168]

In 1791, Hanover Presbytery wrestled with the issue of bringing into the church slaves who lived together but were not legally married. The presbytery solved the problem by reflecting theologically on the nature of marriage. It determined that marriage was constituted "in the sight of God" and by the "mutual consent of the Parties." Therefore if slaves lived a Christian life as a married couple they could be accepted into the church without the legal formality of marriage. This logic was extended also to the issue of divorce. It was determined that if a couple were forcibly separated by the sale or removal of one of the spouses, the remaining slave could take "another Companion" as if "the other were dead" and remain in the church.[169]

The theological precedent of allowing the moral equivalent of death (or adultery, or desertion) to permit divorce and remarriage was used extensively in dealing with divorce and remarriage in the Presbyterian churches from the 1930s onward, and I deal with this below. Whether this attitude drew consciously on the precedent of slave marriage I do not know. However, the same kind of theological reasonings used in the case of slave marriages was later used in dealing with divorce and remarriage for all Presbyterians.

*A Person-Centered Understanding of Divorce
and Remarriage in the PCUSA*

Our current, more person-centered attitude toward divorce and remarriage really began in 1929 when the Presbytery of Dubuque reacted against the attempt by the General Assembly in 1928 to eliminate all exceptions and forbid divorce in all instances. The Dubuque overture noted that a strict legalism would "not solve the problem, but may cause hardship and injustice."[170] Political timing was also an issue here, for the matter arose soon after the 1929 stock market crash and the beginning of the Great Depression, which sensitized Americans to personal and social needs.

In 1930 the PCUSA General Assembly received an extensive study of divorce and remarriage in the church. The 1930 Report of the Commission on Marriage, Divorce, and Remarriage took a spiritual, rather than legalistic, approach to Scripture and the Confessions. The primary texts concerning Jesus' attitude toward divorce, Matthew 19:3–13 and Mark 10:2–12, were presented as ideals that should enable young people to appreciate "the meaning and values of marriage." Numerous New Testament texts were offered to show the desirability of marriage: 1 Corinthians 7; 1 Timothy 3:2, 12; Hebrews 13:4.[171]

The commission report recommended no change in the existing standards that allowed remarriage after divorce only for the innocent party in cases of adultery or irremediable desertion. It offered, however, a spiritual understanding and application of the Westminister Confession and Catechisms. "Beyond the fact that the marriage relation is terminated by death, is the further fact that it may be destroyed by either party to the agreement proving unfaithful to the vows taken."[172] The commission thus concluded: "Anything that kills love and deals death to the spirit of the union is infidelity," citing the biblical phrase, "The letter killeth; but the spirit giveth life."[173] Here the concept of a moral equivalent of death is introduced.

In the context of the above interpretations, the commission recommended that the position of the Westminster Standards (Confession and Catechisms) remain unchanged, that there were only two grounds for divorce, "adultery and irremediable desertion."[174] The meaning of adultery and desertion, however, had been given an expanded spiritual, rather than literal, meaning.

By 1952, a new report of a Special Committee on Proposed Changes in the Confession of Faith stated that "remarriage after a divorced granted on grounds explicitly stated in Scripture or implicit in the gospel of Christ may be sanctioned in keeping with his redemptive gospel."[175]

Revisions to the Westminster Confession of Faith were approved by the presbyteries and adopted by the PCUSA General Assembly in 1953 to allow divorce and remarriage on these theological grounds. The approved overture was careful to express concern for the "establishment of marriage in the Lord as Scripture sets it forth" and with "present penitence" as well as "past innocence or guilt" of those "whose marriage has been broken." The interpretation of Scripture employed both the proof-texting and the christological approaches by approving grounds for remarriage "explicitly stated in Scripture or implicit in the gospel of Christ." A gracious and a legalistic ethos were combined in stating that remarriage could be sanctioned "in keeping with His redemptive gospel," but only "when sufficient penitence for sin and failure is evident, and a firm purpose of and endeavor after Christian marriage is manifest."[176]

A Parallel Change on Divorce and Remarriage in the PCUS

The Southern stream was experiencing a parallel struggle over the matter of divorce and remarriage during the same period. During the 1929 attempt by a PCUS committee to eliminate "desertion" as a ground for divorce, the concept of moral equivalency was introduced. Dr. Charles E. Diehl, then President of Southwestern College in Memphis, argued: "We recognize the violation of the Seventh Commandment *or its moral equivalent* [italics mine] as the only ground for divorce." He went on to say that desertion "and perhaps some other causes constitute what may be termed 'moral equivalent.'"[177]

By 1938, the PCUS Permanent Committee on Moral and Social Welfare noted that "there is a surprising divergence of interpretation of our own Standards in reference to 'desertion.'" It remarked on the wide variety of practice among PCUS ministers regarding marrying or not marrying persons who had been divorced.[178]

In 1945 in the aftermath of the strains of World War II, the PCUS received an overture to conduct a careful study of the laws of the church on grounds for divorce and procedure for remarriage.[179] In 1950, the Council of Christian Relations, which carried on the work of the former Committee on Social and Moral Welfare, submitted its first report on "Divorce and Remarriage." No specific changes in the Westminster Confession were recommended. However, the council presented some important conclusions.

The 1950 report's comments on biblical interpretation reflected the new approach taken in the PCUS since the 1940s.
The council said: "Any attempt to build a Christian doctrine of
marriage and divorce on a few isolated 'proof-texts' will always
fail for at least two reasons: (a) the usual proof-texts are open
to more than one interpretation, and (b) they fail to give due
weight to the implications of Jesus' total teaching with respect
to man's personal responsibilities and social relationships."[180]

Applying this principle to divorce, they commented that
"infidelity can be spiritual as well as physical and it manifests
itself in many forms. It is therefore unrealistic to hold that divorce is permissible only when marriage has been broken by
one of two forms of infidelity, both of which are physical
acts."[181] They concluded: "Wherever free Protestant churches
are studying this problem today in the light of Jesus' total
teachings on human relations, the trend is unmistakably away
from a strictly legalistic approach to one more finely and fun-
damentally spiritual."[182]

A report to the 1952 Assembly, by the PCUS Council on
Christian Relations, stated that limiting grounds for remarriage after divorce to adultery and desertion "may be doing
grave injustice to a multitude of injured people who are victims
of forces they could not control." Moreover, "in practice they
[PCUS ministers] are ignoring the letter of our Church's law
in order, as they see it, to be true to the spirit and total teachings of our Lord, to the practical realities of life and to the de-
mands of Christian justice."[183]

In 1959, after fourteen years of struggle, the PCUS
amended the Westminster Confession of Faith regarding divorce. The presbyteries overwhelmingly approved essential
wording similar to that of their Northern cousins, although it
was hedged with many qualifiers and footnoted with a long list
of Scripture references.[184]

The PCUS wording, now in the PC(USA) *Book of Confessions*, prefaces its change of stance with a lengthy discussion
of the divine intention that "persons entering the marriage
covenant become inseparably united." The rationale for dis-
solving that covenant is "the weaknesses of one or both part-
ners" that "may lead to gross and persistent denial of the

marriage vows so that the marriage dies at the heart and the union becomes intolerable." Then follows wording exactly like that in the PCUSA revised section of Westminster: "The remarriage of divorced persons may be sanctioned by the Church in keeping with the redemptive Gospel of Christ, when sufficient penitence for sin and failure is evident, and a firm purpose of and endeavor after Christian marriage is manifested."[185]

In the 1950s, both branches of American Presbyterianism revised the Westminster Confession of Faith on divorce and remarriage. In both cases, Presbyterians shifted their emphasis from a public norm to personal exceptions. The primary purpose of marriage was reunderstood from being for the benefit of society to being for the benefit of the persons entering the marriage covenant.[186]

From the perspective of interpretation, the Presbyterian denominations turned away from a legalistic approach to marriage and divorce based on a literal interpretation of biblical and confessional texts. Instead, the spirit and totality of Jesus' teaching was cited as mandating a pastoral approach that allowed exceptions to previous rules. Finally, changes were made in the Confession of Faith.

Pondering the Pace of Change

Whereas it took over a century for the church to cope with entrenched injustices to African Americans and women, the church changed its stance on the matter of divorce and remarriage in thirty-three years, between 1926 and 1959. Might it be that one significant difference was that those present and voting in presbyteries and General Assembly were vulnerable to divorce and thus could feel the necessity for change? Regarding racial injustice or women's equality, however, because those voting in presbyteries were all white and all men, they were able to distance themselves from those affected by their decisions. They could treat the problems "objectively" and focus on the good of society in general. But when it touched them, as with all human beings, their concerns become much more personal and pastoral.

c. General Assembly Policy

General Assembly policies affirm the value of seeing any issue in the context of the *Book of Confessions* as a whole. In its confessions, the Presbyterian Church (U.S.A.) "gives witness to the faith of the church catholic";[187] "identifies with the affirmations of the Protestant Reformation";[188] and "expresses the faith of the Reformed tradition."[189] Any confession in the *Book of Confessions* should be compatible with these great traditions.[190]

The report on The Confessional Nature of the Church adds: "General Assemblies, synods, presbyteries, and sessions, as well as individual church officers, should be led, instructed, and continually guided by the whole *Book of Confessions.*"[191]

Conclusion

For Presbyterians, Holy Scripture and the *Book of Confessions* are the primary sources of authority and guidance. Authorities are helpful only if they are correctly interpreted. In this book I have presented denominationally approved guidelines for interpreting Scripture and have also offered parallel guidelines for interpreting the Confessions. I have, in addition, reviewed some of the actual interpretive practices of Presbyterians throughout American history. Presbyterians have discovered that some theories about interpretation have led us into practices that we later had to repent of and repudiate. We no longer cite the Bible to justify the oppression of African Americans, the subordination of women, and the exclusion of divorced and remarried persons. We have reinterpreted and amended our Confessions and written new affirmations of faith that have recorded our commitments to the equality of all God's people.

We have discovered some ways of interpreting Scripture and the Confessions that better accord with our ordination vows and constitutional standards. Jesus Christ is the center of our faith. The attitudes and teachings of Jesus Christ are our best interpreter of Scripture and the Confessions. The early Christian church discovered that it had to interpret its source of authority and guidance, the Old Testament. Literalism would not do. Neither would claims to private revelation. Christians had to use the plain text of Scripture, but they read it through the lens of their experience of Jesus Christ.

Everyone interprets. The truth is not always and immediately obvious. We can have knowledge that is adequate but not always technically perfect. The Bible is useful, but for what? Scripture teaches that its purpose is to give us knowledge that leads to salvation in Christ and a life of Christian service. The Reformed tradition is clear that the purpose of Scripture is to give us practical knowledge of how to be Christians, rather than theoretical knowledge about other matters that we can get in other ways.

In the history of American Presbyterianism we have not always gotten our interpretation right. Due to historical circumstances, a tradition of biblical interpretation dominated in the nineteenth century that we have since then had to reject. We felt great pressure to compete with Post-Reformation Roman Catholicism and the rise of scientific criticism of Scripture. Under that pressure, some Presbyterian theologians developed theories of interpretation that diverged greatly from that of Calvin, the sixteenth-century Reformers, and the Westminster Divines. Our nineteenth-century predecessors attempted to prove that the Bible was technically perfect as literature and a reliable guide in matters of science. They claimed that what the Bible said was what God had said, and thus no interpretation was necessary. They called the Bible an inerrant book.

The assumption that the meaning of the Bible was obvious unfortunately allowed theologians and church members to read into it the biases of their nineteenth-century culture. Good, intelligent, and devout Presbyterian theologians argued against emancipating slaves and allowing women to vote. They read the mores of their society back into Scripture.

Their theory of biblical inerrancy led them to require particular proof-texts either to commend or to deny particular practices. They lost sight of the fact that the Bible was written in an ancient, Near Eastern culture. And they turned away from the great themes of Scripture: love God and love your neighbor; God makes all things new in Jesus Christ. Instead, the Bible became a book of discrete statements that they called facts.

A revival of interest in Calvin and the sixteenth-century Reformation that began in the 1930s took hold in seminaries in the 1940s and presented American Presbyterians with a new option—all of Scripture should be interpreted by looking at it through our experience of Jesus Christ. Scripture really becomes the Word of God to us only when the Holy Spirit opens our minds and hearts to the message of the gospel of Christ. A new, christological approach to interpretation, more in harmony with Calvin, took hold in American Presbyterianism. It enabled us finally to accept changes in attitude toward race, gender, and roles in society that we had resisted in the previous century.

Since the mid–twentieth century we have worked to understand Scripture more in its original setting and then to think creatively about how it can apply in our context. We have been freed from treating our Confessions as if they were exact replicas of the Bible. We have reinterpreted and added to our Confessions. And we have written new affirmations of faith that more adequately apply the gospel in our situation.

This study of the church's historical practices of interpretation has yielded some warnings about blind alleys not to take. When we try to claim essential status for our interpretations, inferences, or applications of Scripture, we are in danger of becoming sectarian, of fostering splinter groups, or of absolutizing theological schools of thought.

Past practices have also suggested new possibilities for creative applications of the Confessions. We have observed that the essentials of the faith lie in the broad themes, the great doctrines of Scripture and the Confessions on which we all agree. The church has applied one issue in a past confession to a new issue in the present time, just as the Confession of 1967's attitude toward racial reconciliation served as a platform for affirming the equality of women and men. Even the example of how slave marriages were dealt with in the eighteenth century provided a concept of "moral equivalency" that enabled us in the 1950s to develop a more biblical approach to divorce and remarriage.

The seven guidelines for interpreting Scripture and the Confessions that I have outlined can be enormously helpful to us as contemporary Presbyterians. We will not always agree on their precise application. But at least we can all be on the same page in the discussion! It will be very useful, as future controversies arise, for all parties involved to reflect on Scripture and review the Confessions remembering these principles:

1. Jesus Christ with his redemptive gospel is the central theme of Scripture and the Confessions.
2. Our focus should be on the plain text of Scripture and the Confessions in their grammatical, historical, and cultural context.
3. We should depend on the guidance of the Holy Spirit to lead us into clearer and more complete understandings of Scripture and the Confessions.
4. We should be guided by the great themes of Scripture that are the confessional consensus of the church.
5. All of our interpretations should be in accord with the rule of love that commands love of God and neighbor and commends the redeeming love of Christ.
6. The church needs to do careful study of the Bible and the Confessions in their original historical and cultural context and then discern their appropriate theological application in our day.
7. Each particular passage of the Bible and the Confessions needs to be interpreted in the light of the whole message of Scripture.

We have a great opportunity to use our historical sources of authority and guidance creatively in the present. The great themes of Scripture found in the Confessions are nourishing and necessary for living a contemporary, Reformed, Christian life. The Confessions orient us to the Reformed and Presbyterian heritage as understood by our foreparents in the faith. They were reformers who made new pastoral and practical applications of their ancient heritage. They did not slavishly follow the customs of their predecessors. We are not obliged to replicate their culture or customs. We do them injustice if we use their gifts to us literalistically and legalistically.

We must radically respect the caution given in the Westminster Confession of Faith:

All synods or councils since the apostles' times, whether general or particular, may err, and many have erred; therefore they are not to be made the rule of faith or practice, but to be used as a help in both.[1]

Our task is to think theologically about how best to apply the intentions of our forebears to live out the gospel of Christ in their time. We need to heed their warning that the Confessions are not a rule but a help. Then we must have the courage, as they did, to apply Christ's message in our own time and context.

NOTES

Introduction: Interpreting Scripture and the Confessions

1. *Book of Order* G-14.0207c; hereafter *BO*.
2. Roland G. Tharp and Ronald Gallimore, "Basketball's John Wooden: What a Coach Can Teach a Teacher," *Psychology Today* 9, no. 8 (January 1976): 75–78. Wooden's personal, almost parental relationship to his players no doubt also made his more didactic correction effective.
3. *BO*, G-6.0106b.

Part 1: Interpreting an Authoritative Scripture

1. Edward Reynolds, "Israel's Prayer in Time of Trouble, with God's Gracious Answer Thereunto; or an Explication of the Fourteenth Chapter of the Prophet Hosea, in Seven Sermons, Preached upon So Many Days of Solemn Humiliation [1645]," in *The Whole Works of the Right Reverend Edward Reynolds* (London: J. R. Pitman, 1826), 412–13, cited in Jack Bartlett Rogers, *Scripture in the Westminster Confession: A Problem of Historical Interpretation for American Presbyterianism* (Grand Rapids: Eerdmans, 1967), 370–71.

Chapter 1: Everyone Interprets

1. See John Goldingay, *Models for Interpretation of Scripture* (Grand Rapids: Eerdmans, 1995), 2–3.
2. Donald W. Musser and Joseph L. Price, eds., *A New Handbook of Christian Theology* (Nashville: Abingdon Press, 1992), s.v. "Hermeneutics."
3. See John Barton, *How the Bible Came to Be* (Louisville: Westminster John Knox Press, 1998).
4. Jack B. Rogers and Donald K. McKim, *The Authority and Interpretation of the Bible: An Historical Approach* (San Francisco: Harper & Row, 1979), 4–5; hereafter *AIB*.

5. V. See *The French Confession of 1559* (Louisville: The Office of Theology and Worship, Presbyterian Church [U.S.A.], 1998), 6.
6. *Book of Confessions*, 5.002; hereafter *BC*.
7. *BC*, 6.001, 6.002.
8. *BC*, 9.06.
9. *BC*, 10.1.
10. *BC*, 10.4

Chapter 2: Presbyterian Policy on Interpreting Scripture

1. The two reports are available in one booklet from Distribution Management Services in Louisville (DMS Order #OGA-92-003).
2. Comments from a personal conversation with the chair of the committee.
3. "Report of the Committee on Pluralism in the Church to the 190th General Assembly (1978) of the United Presbyterian Church in the United States of America," *Minutes*, 1978, Part I, p. 293.
4. *Presbyterian Understanding and Use of Holy Scripture and Biblical Authority and Interpretation* (Louisville: Office of the General Assembly, 1992), Preface.
5. *Biblical Authority and Interpretation*, A Resource Document Received by the 194th General Assembly (1982) of the United Presbyterian Church in the United States of America (Louisville: Office of the General Assembly, 1992), 29–33.
6. *Biblical Authority and Interpretation*, 30.
7. *Biblical Authority and Interpretation*, 30 and 33.
8. Donald K. McKim, ed. *Westminster Dictionary of Theological Terms* (Louisville: Westminster John Knox Press, 1996), s.v. "scholasticism, Protestant"; hereafter *Dictionary*.
9. Calvin, *Institutes*, I.ix.3, cited in Rogers and McKim, *AIB*, 106: "But those who wish to prove to unbelievers that Scripture is the Word of God are acting foolishly, for only by faith can this be known."
10. Rogers and McKim, *AIB*, 172–84.
11. Ibid., 235.
12. Ibid., 235–47.
13. Ibid., 268–69.
14. Karlfried Froehlich, "'Abinadab's Chariot': The Predicament of Biblical Interpretation," *The Princeton Seminary Bulletin* XVIII (1997): 265.
15. Charles Hodge, *Systematic Theology*, Vol. I, p. 10, cited in Rogers and McKim, *AIB*, 293.

16. See Rogers and McKim, *AIB*, 375 n. 144.

17. *Biblical Authority and Interpretation*, 43.

18. McKim, *Dictionary*, s.v. "fundamentalist modernist controversy."

19. *Biblical Authority and Interpretation*, 36–38.

20. McKim, *Dictionary*, s.v. "Neo-Orthodoxy."

21. For a recent exposition and appraisal of the thought of Barth, Brunner, and five other theologians usually designated as Neo-Orthodox, see Douglas John Hall, *Remembered Voices: Reclaiming the Legacy of "Neo-Orthodoxy"* (Louisville: Westminster John Knox Press, 1998).

22. McKim, *Dictionary*, s.v. "Kierkegaardian."

23. *Biblical Authority and Interpretation*, 38–44.

24. *BC*, 9.27.

25. Jack Rogers, "Biblical Authority and Confessional Change," *Journal of Presbyterian History* 59, no. 2 (Summer 1981): 136–37.

26. *The Confessional Statement of the United Presbyterian Church of North America* (Pittsburgh: Board of Christian Education of the United Presbyterian Church of North America, 1951), Article III, "Of Holy Scripture," p. 9.

27. *Report of the Special Committee on a Brief Contemporary Statement of Faith to the 177th General Assembly, the United Presbyterian Church in the United States of America, May 1965* (Philadelphia: Office of the General Assembly, 1965), 29, cited in Rogers, "Biblical Authority and Confessional Change," 142; hereafter *Report*.

28. *Report*, 1965, cited in Rogers, "Biblical Authority and Confessional Change," 142.

29. Ibid., 142–43.

30. See McKim, *Dictionary*, s.v. "Neo-Orthodoxy"; and Musser and Price, *A New Handbook*, s.v. "Neoorthodoxy."

31. Cf. James H. Moorhead, "Redefining Confessionalism: American Presbyterians in the Twentieth Century," in *The Confessional Mosaic: Presbyterians and Twentieth-Century Theology*, eds. Milton J Coalter, John M. Mulder, and Louis B. Weeks (Louisville: Westminster John Knox Press, 1990), 66.

32. McKim, *Dictionary*, s.v. "context," "contextual," and "contextual theology."

33. McKim, *Dictionary*, s.v. "existentialism, Christian."

34. *Biblical Authority and Interpretation*, 41–43.

35. On Origen, see Rogers and McKim, *AIB*, 12; and for Calvin, see Rogers and McKim, *AIB*, 98–99 and 108.

36. See Rogers and McKim, *AIB*, 108.

37. *Biblical Authority and Interpretation*, 43–44.

Chapter 3: Seven Guidelines for Interpreting Scripture in Matters of Controversy

1. See *Biblical Authority and Interpretation*, 44–45 and 52–53.

2. Cited in *Presbyterian Understanding and Use of Holy Scripture and Biblical Authority and Interpretation*. Position Statement adopted by the 123rd General Assembly (1983) of the Presbyterian Church in the United States (Louisville: Office of the General Assembly, 1992), 17.

3. *BC*, 3.18.

4. *BC*, 8.11.

5. *BC*, 9.29.

6. Edward John Carnell, *The Case for Orthodox Theology* (Philadelphia: The Westminster Press, 1959), 113. For a discussion of the relationship of fundamentalism to evangelicalism, see Jack Rogers, *Claiming the Center: Churches and Conflicting Worldviews* (Louisville: Westminster John Knox Press, 1995), 72–74. For a more detailed, recent account of the relationship between fundamentalism and evangelicalism, see Gary Dorrien, *The Remaking of Evangelical Theology* (Louisville: Westminster John Knox Press, 1998).

7. Carnell, *The Case for Orthodox Theology*, 57–64.

8. The material has been officially adopted by our denomination. See James E. Davison, *The Year of the Bible: A Comprehensive, Congregation-Wide Program of Bible Reading* (Louisville: Bridge Resources, 1996).

9. Luke 4:18–19. Cf. Isa. 61:1–12 and 58:6.

10. *Presbyterian Understanding and Use*, 11–12.

11. Calvin, *Institutes of the Christian Religion*, IV.xvi.23, cited in Rogers and McKim, *AIB*, 97.

12. *BC*, 5.010.

13. *BC*, 9.27, 29.

14. C. S. Lewis, *Reflections on the Psalms* (London: Geoffrey Bles, 1958), 112.

15. General Assembly *Minutes*, 1916, pp. 76, 80A; hereafter *Minutes*, PCUS. Cited in Lois A. Boyd and R. Douglas Brackenridge, *Presbyterian Women in America: Two Centuries of a Quest for Status*. Contributions to the Study of Religion, No. 9. A Publication of the Presbyterian Historical Society (Westport, Conn.: Greenwood Press, 1983), 211–12.

16. *BC*, 6.006.

17. *BC*, 6.010.

18. *BC*, 9.30.

19. "Report of the Ad Interim Committee on a Biblical Study of the Position of Women in the Church" (*Minutes*, PCUS, 1956), p. 141.

20. See also Isa. 65:17.

21. John 14:26; 16:12–14.

22. *BC*, 4.022.

23. *Presbyterian Understanding and Use*, 21.

24. *BC*, 5.010.

25. *Presbyterian Understanding and Use*, 20.

26. *BC*, 5.010.

27. *BC*, 3.18.

28. John W. Christie and Dwight Dumond, *George Bourne and The Book and Slavery Irreconcilable*, Presbyterian Historical Society Series, Vol. IX (Wilmington, Del.: The Historical Society of Delaware, 1969), 61.

29. *Address of the General Assembly of the Presbyterian Church in the Confederate States of America to All the Churches of Jesus Christ Throughout the Earth, Adopted Unanimously at the Organization of the General Assembly in Augusta, Ga., December, 1861* (N.p.: Published by order of the Assembly, n.d.).

30. Harriet Beecher Stowe, *Uncle Tom's Cabin or Life Among the Lowly* (Boston: Houghton, Mifflin & Co., 1851).

31. *Extract from Minutes of the General Assembly*, 1803–1811, p. 310, cited in Karen (Bear) Ride Scott, "Expanding the Horizons of Ministry: Women of the Cloth in the Presbyterian Church, U.S.A." (D. Min. diss. project, San Francisco Theological Seminary, 1990), 84.

32. Boyd and Brackenridge, *Presbyterian Women in America*, 6.

33. Ronald W. Hogeland, "Charles Hodge, The Association of Gentlemen and Ornamental Womanhood: 1825–1855," *Journal of Presbyterian History* 53, no. 3 (Fall 1975): 242.

34. African Americans and women have provided substantial resources to enable others to benefit from their insights into biblical interpretation. See, for example: Cain Hope Felder, ed., *Stony the Road We Trod: African American Biblical Interpretation* (Minneapolis: Fortress Press, 1991); Letty M. Russell, ed., *Feminist Interpretation of the Bible* (Philadelphia: The Westminster Press, 1985).

35. *BC*, 6.007.

36. *BC*, 6.007.

37. *BC*, 6.008.

38. Cited in *Presbyterian Understanding and Use*, 22.

39. *BC*, 6.175.

40. Regarding the attitude of the Westminster Divines toward: (1) Resisting putting proof-texts to their Confession, see Rogers, *Scripture in the Westminster Confession*, 176–77; (2) Not recommending

memorizing the Shorter Catechism, see S. W. Carruthers, *Three Centuries of the Westminster Shorter Catechism*, with a Facsimile Reproduction of the Original Manuscript Presented to Parliament, 25th November, 1647 (Fredericton, New Brunswick: University of New Brunswick, 1957), 7; (3) not intending that the Westminster Confession be subscribed as church law, see *BC*, 6.175. For further background: Rogers, *Scripture in the Westminster Confession*, 200, and Leonard J. Trinterud, *The Forming of An American Tradition: A Reexamination of Colonial Presbyterianism* (Philadelphia: The Westminster Press, 1949), 39–44.

41. Walter Goldschmidt, *Comparative Functionalism* (Berkeley: University of California Press, 1966), 134, cited in Charles H. Kraft, *Christianity in Culture: A Study in Dynamic Biblical Theologizing in Cross-Cultural Perspective* (Maryknoll, N.Y.: Orbis Books, 1979), 84.

42. 1 Thess. 5:26; 2 Cor. 13:12.

43. John 13:14.

44. See "Report . . . Women in the Church," *Minutes*, PCUS, 1956, p. 141.

45. *BC*, 5.010.

46. *BC*, 6.009.

47. Rogers, *Claiming the Center*, 2–3.

48. Ernest Trice Thompson, *Presbyterians in the South, Volume Two: 1861–1890* (Richmond: John Knox Press, 1973), 218.

49. Robert L. Dabney, "Anti-Biblical Theories of Rights," *Presbyterian Quarterly* 2, no. 2 (July 1888): 217, 219.

50. For another helpful, contemporary approach, see John P. Burgess, *Why Scripture Matters: Reading the Bible in a Time of Church Conflict* (Louisville: Westminster John Knox Press, 1998).

Part 2: Interpreting the Reformed Confessions

1. Volume iii, p. 157, cited in John Lightfoot, *The Whole Works of the Rev. John Lightfoot, D.D.*, ed. the Rev. John Rogers Pitman, A.M., Vol. XIII, Containing The Journal of the Proceedings of the Assembly of Divines: from January 1, 1643, to December 31, 1644, and Letters to and from Dr. Lightfoot (London: J. F. Dove, St. John's Square, 1824). For a discussion of this vow in its various forms, see Rogers, *Scripture in the Westminster Confession*, 126–28.

Chapter 4: How to Interpret the *Book of Confessions*

1. "The Confessional Nature of the Church," Commended to the Church for Study by the 198th General Assembly (1986) Presby-

terian Church (U.S.A.) (Louisville: Theology and Worship Ministry Unit, 1986), 29.113.

2. Ibid., 29.116.

3. Ibid.

4. Jack Rogers, *Presbyterian Creeds: A Guide to the Book of Confessions* (Louisville: Westminster John Knox Press, 1985; rev. ed., 1991).

5. See also Harry W. Eberts, Jr., *We Believe: A Study of the Book of Confessions for Church Officers* (Philadelphia: Geneva Press, 1987).

6. Edward A. Dowey, Jr., *A Commentary on the Confession of 1967 and An Introduction to the Book of Confessions* (Philadelphia: The Westminster Press, 1968).

7. Dowey, *Commentary*, 273–75. Dowey's model was *The Harmony of Protestant Confessions*, produced in 1581, which used the Second Helvetic Confession, the most extensive of the sixteenth-century confessions, as the framework.

8. Jan Rohls, *Reformed Confessions: Theology from Zurich to Barmen*, trans. John Hoffmeyer. Columbia Series in Reformed Theology (Louisville: Westminster John Knox Press, 1998).

9. *BO*, G-14.0207.

10. I will deal with this concept of "essential tenets" more extensively in Chapter 6 under the "Rule of Faith."

11. Note 1 states that "The preface and the appendix do not have confessional authority."

12. *BO*, G-2.0500.

13. *BC*, 10.3, 11. 29–30.

14. *BC*, 10.3, 11. 42–43.

15. *BC*, 10.3, 1.48.

16. *BC*, 10.3, 1.38.

17. H. Richard Niebuhr, *Christ and Culture* (New York: Harper & Brothers, 1951).

18. *BC*, 3.24.

19. *BC*, 3.24.

20. *BC*, 3.14.

21. See Kraft, *Christianity in Culture*, 91.

22. Ibid., 53.

23. Ibid., 46.

24. *BC*, 7.249.

Chapter 5: General Assembly Policies Regarding Interpretation of the Confessions

1. For further discussion of Presbyterian polity, see Joan S. Gray and Joyce C. Tucker, *Presbyterian Polity for Church Officers*, 3d ed. (Louisville: Geneva Press, 1998), and Clifton Kirkpatrick and

William H. Hopper, Jr., *What Unites Presbyterians: Common Ground for Troubled Times* (Louisville: Geneva Press, 1997), chap. 11. See the foundational principles of Presbyterian church order in the *Book of Order*, especially: *BO*, G-1.0400; G-4.0301; G-4.0303; G-4.0304; G-7.0103.

    2. *BO*, G-14.0207.

    3. *BO*, G-2010.

    4. As this book was being prepared, the Advisory Committee on the *Constitution*, at the direction of the General Assembly, was engaged in drafting a revision of the *Book of Order*. In some instances, material has been rearranged and slightly reworded. I have followed the proposed revision, but included the citations to the earlier form of the *Book of Order*. See *BO*, G-2.0100 and G-2.0500b.

    5. *BO*, G-2.0200.

    6. *BO*, G-2.0500b.

    7. "Confessional Nature."

    8. "Confessional Nature," 12. The guidelines are as follows: (1) "General Assemblies, synods, presbyteries, and sessions, as well as individual church officers, should be led, instructed, and continually guided by the whole Book of Confessions." 29.205. (2) "The confessions of the Book of Confessions are standards, in response to the historical context of the time, which are subordinate to Scripture; they are subject to criticism in light of the word of God in Jesus Christ as witnessed in the Scriptures of the Old and New Testaments and may be revised by the Church following duly prescribed procedures." 29.206. (3) "The confessions are serious statements and are 'not to be taken lightly.' While neither the General Assembly nor any presbytery or session should demand adherence to any specific list of beliefs or doctrinal formulations as if the content of the faith could be reduced to a few selected and precisely worded statements of doctrine, General Assemblies, synods, presbyteries, and sessions have the responsibility of determining on a case by case basis whether candidates for ordination adhere to the standards of doctrine set out in the confessions." 29.207. (4) "When individuals or groups in the church call into question some aspect of the confessions or of the church's interpretation of them, those who hear that objective should consider the possibility that the dispute may point to a deficiency in present confessional standards, remembering that, indeed, synods or councils may err and that the church is always to be reformed (semper reformanda). However, after due consideration, the court of jurisdiction must decide whether such objection is to be allowed to stand or is to be ruled as being out of conformity with the confessional standards of the church." 29.208. (5) "Thus, when individuals or groups in the church persist in dis-

agreeing with the confessions or the church's interpretation of them, the appropriate church body has the responsibility of determining whether the disagreement is sufficient to prevent the approval of a candidate for ordination to the office of pastor, elder, or deacon." 29.209. (6) "So long as presbyteries do not contradict specific interpretations of the confessions made by the General Assembly, and so long as sessions do not contradict those made by the Assembly and their presbytery, presbyteries and sessions have the right and responsibility to interpret for themselves whether candidates for ordination and ordained persons, for whom they are responsible, hold to the 'essentials' of the faith as articulated by the confessions of the church (the constitutional right of appeal being understood)." 29.210.

9. "The Assessment of Proposed Amendments to *The Book of Confessions*" (Louisville: Office of Theology and Worship, 1997), 1.

10. Ibid., 5.

Chapter 6: Guidelines for Interpreting the *Book of Confessions*

1. See Chapter 5 for further detail.

2. Robert Ellis Thompson, *A History of the Presbyterian Churches in the United States*, The American Church History Series, Vol. VI (New York: The Christian Literature Co., 1895), 362–63; John Robinson, *The Testimony and Practice of the Presbyterian Church in Reference to American Slavery with an Appendix: Containing the Position of the General Assembly (New School), Free Presbyterian Church, Reformed Presbyterian, Associate, Associate Reformed, Baptist, Protestant Episcopal, and Methodist Episcopal Churches* (Cincinnati: John D. Thorpe, 1852), 16–17.

3. Robinson, *The Testimony and Practice*, 35.

4. Ibid.

5. James Henley Thornwell, "The Relation of the Church to Slavery," in *The Collected Writings of James Henley Thornwell*, Vol. 4 (Edinburgh: Banner of Truth Trust, 1974; original publication 1875), 385, cited in Ronald C. White, Jr., "Social Witness and Evangelism," chapter 7 of *How Shall We Witness? Faithful Evangelism in a Reformed Tradition*, ed. Milton J Coalter and Virgil Cruz (Louisville: Westminster John Knox Press, 1995), 140. See also E. T. Thompson, Vol. 2, p. 30.

6. Robinson, *The Testimony and Practice*, 35, 36.

7. Ibid., 37.

8. Ernest Trice Thompson, *Presbyterians in the South, Volume One: 1607–1861* (Richmond: John Knox Press, 1963), 530.

9. Cited in James Oscar Farmer, Jr., *The Metaphysical Confederacy:*

James Henley Thornwell and the Synthesis of Southern Values (Macon, Ga.: Mercer University Press, 1986), 222.

10. *Address . . . 1861*, 11.

11. Ibid., 12.

12. Ibid.

13. Ernest Trice Thompson, *Presbyterians in the South, Volume Three: 1890–1972* (Richmond: John Knox Press, 1973), 493–94.

14. Ibid., 494. See also John M. Mulder and Lee A. Wyatt, "The Predicament of Pluralism: The Study of Theology in Presbyterian Seminaries Since the 1920s," in *The Pluralistic Vision: Presbyterians and Mainstream Protestant Education and Leadership*, ed. Milton J Coalter, John M. Mulder, and Louis B. Weeks (Louisville: Westminster John Knox Press, 1992), 43–44, 48.

15. See Chapter 2 for a definition and explanation of Neo-Orthodoxy.

16. W. Eugene March, "'Biblical Theology,' Authority and the Presbyterians," *Journal of Presbyterian History* 59, no. 2 (Summer 1981): 118.

17. Their counterparts in the North included G. Ernest Wright, Floyd V. Filson, James D. Smart, John Wick Bowman, John A. Mackay, Joseph Haroutuian, and Otto Piper. See March, "'Biblical Theology,'" 118.

18. March, "'Biblical Theology,'" 119.

19. Ibid., 121.

20. Ibid., 121–22.

21. E. T. Thompson, Vol. 3, 539.

22. Ibid.

23. Ibid., 540.

24. "Report . . . Women," *Minutes*, PCUS, 1956, p. 141.

25. Marthame E. Sanders III, "'A Fellowship of Concern,' and the Declining Doctrine of the Spirituality of the Church in the Presbyterian Church in the United States," *Journal of Presbyterian History* 75, no. 3 (Fall 1997): 182.

26. Ibid., 184–85.

27. *BC*, 9.27.

28. Dowey, *Commentary*, 40–41.

29. *BC*, 9.44.

30. "A Declaration of Faith (Presbyterian Church in the United States)" in *The Proposed Book of Confessions with Related Documents*. Approved by the 116th General Assembly and Recommended to the Presbyteries for Their Advice and Consent (Atlanta: Presbyterian Church in the United States, 1976), chap. 6, 11. 65–67.

31. "Declaration of Faith," chap. 2, 11. 122–25.

32. *BO*, G-2.0200.

33. "Confessional Nature," 10, at 29.206 (c).
34. WCF, 1646, Chapter XXIV, III in *The Confession of Faith of the Assembly of Divines at Westminster, From the Original Manuscript Written by Cornelius Burges in 1646*, ed. S. W. Carruthers (N.p.: Presbyterian Church of England, 1946).
35. *BC*, 6.145, n. u.
36. *BC*, 7.249.
37. *BC*, 5.24.
38. *BC*, 7.061; 7.229.
39. *BC*, 7.249.
40. *BC*, 7.249.
41. *BC*, 7.219.
42. *BC*, 5.217.
43. *BC*, 6.114.
44. *Minutes*, PCUSA, 1930, p. 87.
45. *BC*, 6.145, n. u.
46. *BC*, 6.131, n. q.
47. *BC*, 6.009. Cited in "Report . . . Women," *Minutes*, PCUS, 1956, p. 139.
48. "Report . . . Women," *Minutes*, PCUS, 1956, p. 139.
49. *BO*, G-2.0500.
50. "Confessional Nature," p. 5 at 29.151.
51. E. T. Thompson, Vol. 3, p. 214.
52. Maurice W. Armstrong, Lefferts A. Loetscher, and Charles A. Anderson, eds., *The Presbyterian Enterprise: Sources of American Presbyterian History* (Philadelphia: The Westminster Press, 1956), 247. Supralapsarianism is the doctrine that God has decreed even before creation who will be saved and who will be lost. See Donald K. McKim, ed., *Encyclopedia of the Reformed Faith* (Louisville: Westminster John Knox Press, 1992), s.v. "supralapsarianism."
53. Armstrong et al., *The Presbyterian Enterprise*, 247.
54. E. T. Thompson, Vol. 3, pp. 219–20.
55. Armstrong et al., *The Presbyterian Enterprise*, 268.
56. Ibid., 269.
57. E. T. Thompson, Vol. 3, pp. 492–93. See James H. Smylie, *A Brief History of the Presbyterians* (Louisville: Geneva Press, 1996), 99.
58. Smylie, *A Brief History*, 99.
59. Armstrong et al., *The Presbyterian Enterprise*, 289.
60. E. T. Thompson, Vol. 3, p. 336.
61. Ibid., 338.
62. Ibid., 494.
63. *BO*, G-2.0200.
64. "Confessional Nature," p. 10 at 29.206 (b).
65. "Confessional Nature," p. 10 at 29.208 (d).

66. Smylie, *A Brief History*, 45.
67. Quoted in *Minutes*, PCUSA, 1926, p. 74.
68. Armstrong et al., *The Presbyterian Enterprise*, 27.
69. Ibid., 28.
70. Ibid., 31–32.
71. Rogers, *Claiming the Center*, 15–16.
72. McKim, *Dictionary*, s.v. "fundamentalism/fundamentalist and fundamentalist-modernist controversy."
73. McKim, *Dictionary*, s.v. "liberal theology/liberalism" and s.v. "modernism."
74. McKim, *Dictionary*, s.v. "higher criticism."
75. Rogers and McKim, *AIB*, 348–58.
76. Ibid., 358–59.
77. Ibid., 360.
78. Ibid., 361.
79. *Minutes*, PCUSA, 1910, p. 271.
80. Ibid., 272.
81. Ibid., 272–73.
82. Rogers, *Presbyterian Creeds*, 205–6. Non-Presbyterian Fundamentalists usually changed Point 3 from the virgin birth to the deity of Christ, and made Christ's premillennial second coming Point 5.
83. Ibid., 206.
84. Ibid., 206–7.
85. See Charles E. Quick, "A Statistical Analysis of the Signers of the Auburn Affirmation," *Journal of Presbyterian History* 43, no. 3 (Fall 1965): 182–96, especially pp. 183 and 193. See also Charles E. Quick, "Origins of the Auburn Affirmation," *Journal of Presbyterian History* 53, no. 2 (Summer 1955): 120–42.
86. "An Affirmation designed to safeguard the unity and liberty of the Presbyterian Church in the United States of America," Auburn, N.Y., n.d., p. 3.
87. "An Affirmation," 6. See Rogers and McKim, *AIB*, 364–65.
88. *Minutes*, PCUSA, 1925, p. 88.
89. Rogers, *Claiming the Center*, 31. See also Rogers and McKim, *AIB*, 365.
90. Rogers, *Presbyterian Creeds*, 207.
91. *Minutes*, PCUSA, 1926, p. 72.
92. Ibid., 78–79.
93. *Minutes*, PCUSA, 1927, p. 78.
94. Ibid., 78–79.
95. Ibid., 79–80.
96. Ibid., 81.
97. *BO*, G-2.000–2.0500.
98. *BC*, 10.3, 1. 38.

99. *BO*, G-14.0207e.
100. *BO*, G-2.0200.
101. Rogers and McKim, *AIB*, 275.
102. Ibid., 277.
103. Hogeland, "Charles Hodge," 214.
104. Ibid., 245.
105. Ibid., 248.
106. Jack Rogers, "The Kenyon Case," in *Women and Men in Ministry*, ed. Roberta Hestenes (Pasadena: Fuller Theological Seminary, 1985), 148.
107. Ibid.
108. Ibid., 157–58.
109. Ibid., 161.
110. Ibid., 150.
111. *BC*, 9.44.
112. Rogers, "Kenyon Case," 150.
113. Cf. David B. McCarthy, "Walter Wynn Kenyon (1948–)," in *Dictionary of Heresy Trials in American Christianity*, ed. George H. Shriver (Westport, Conn.: Greenwood Press, 1997).
114. Rogers, *Presbyterian Creeds*, 231–32.
115. *BC*, 10.3.
116. *BC*, 3.22 and 5.191.
117. Rogers, *Presbyterian Creeds*, 248.
118. *BC*, 10.4.
119. *BC*, 10.3.
120. Rogers, *Presbyterian Creeds*, 268–69.
121. *BO*, G-2.0100.
122. "Confessional Nature," p. 11 at 29.210 (f).
123. *BC*, 7.238.
124. *BC*, 7.240.
125. *BC*, 7.242.
126. Mark A. Noll, "The Bible and Slavery," in *Religion and the American Civil War*, ed. Randall M. Miller, Harry S. Stout, and Charles Reagan Wilson (New York: Oxford University Press, 1998), 63.
127. *Address . . . 1861*, 5.
128. Ibid., 11.
129. Ibid., 15.
130. Ibid.
131. Ibid., 14–15.
132. Ibid., 14.
133. Noll, "The Bible and Slavery," 63.
134. Christie and Dumond, *George Bourne*, 17–18.
135. E. T. Thompson, Vol. 1, p. 328.

136. Christie and Dumond, *George Bourne*, 22–23; E. T. Thompson, Vol. 1, p. 329.
137. Robinson, *The Testimony*, 20–21.
138. Christie and Dumond, *George Bourne*, 103.
139. Ibid., 35 and 57; E. T. Thompson, Vol. 1, p. 330.
140. E. T. Thompson, Vol. 1, p. 331; Christie and Dumond, *George Bourne*, 61.
141. Robinson, *The Testimony*, 29–31; E. T. Thompson, Vol. 1, p. 334. Thompson refers to this as a "false lead which diverted the good will of many earnest Christians from more promising solutions."
142. Robinson, *The Testimony*, 32.
143. R. E. Thompson, *A History*, 363.
144. Ibid., 369; James Brown Scouller, *History of the United Presbyterian Church of North America*, in *A History of The Methodist Church, South; The United Presbyterian Church; The Cumberland Presbyterian Church and The Presbyterian Church, South in the United States*, ed. Gross Alexander, James B. Scouller, R. V. Foster, and T. C. Johnson, The American Church History Series, Vol. XI (New York: The Christian Literature Co., 1894), 178.
145. *BC*, 9.46.
146. *BC*, 10.3, 11. 29–31.
147. *BO*, G-2.0200.
148. The *Book of Confessions* has an excellent topical index in the back. One can now purchase the *Book of Confessions* on a CD Rom and use it to do computer word searches.
149. *BC*, 4.022.
150. *BC*, 5.018.
151. *BC*, 7.110.
152. *BC*, 4.108.
153. *BC*, 5.246.
154. *BC*, 5.248.
155. *BC*, 6.137, n. q. (WCF, 1647, XXIV, VI).
156. *BC*, 7.49.
157. *BC*, 7.48.
158. *BC*, 9.44–46.
159. *BC*, 9.47.
160. *BC*, 9.47.
161. Benton Johnson, "From Old to New Agendas: Presbyterians and Social Issues in the Twentieth Century," in *The Confessional Mosaic: Presbyterians and Twentieth-Century Theology*, eds. Milton J Coalter, John M. Mulder, and Louis B. Weeks (Westminster John Knox Press, 1990), 220.
162. *Minutes*, PCUSA, 1930, p. 86.

163. James G. Emerson, Jr., "The Remarriage of Divorced Persons in the United Presbyterian Church of the United States of America" (Ph.D. diss., Divinity School of the University of Chicago, 1959), 124–26; see *Minutes*, PCUS, 1938, p. 110.

164. Emerson, "The Remarriage," 132–33.

165. *Minutes*, PCUS, 1956, 136–37.

166. E. T. Thompson, Vol. 3, 518.

167. Buckley, Thomas E., S. J., "*The Great Catastrophe of My Life*": *Divorce in the Old South.* (Unpublished Manuscript, 1998), 115.

168. Ibid., 118.

169. Ibid.

170. *Minutes*, PCUSA, 1929, cited in Emerson, "The Remarriage," 125.

171. *Minutes*, PCUSA, 1930, pp. 86–87.

172. Ibid., 87.

173. Ibid., 88.

174. Ibid.

175. James G. Emerson, Jr., *Divorce, the Church, and Remarriage* (Philadelphia: The Westminster Press, 1961), 127.

176. *Minutes*, PCUSA, 1953, pp. 43–44. Cf. *BC*, 6.132.

177. *Minutes*, PCUS, 1938, p. 110. Cf. E. T. Thompson, Vol. 3, p. 516.

178. *Minutes*, PCUS, 1938, pp. 111–12.

179. *Minutes*, PCUS, 1946, p. 104.

180. *Minutes*, PCUS, 1953, p. 89.

181. Ibid., 90.

182. Ibid.

183. Ibid.

184. *Minutes*, PCUS, 1959, pp. 68–70; E. T. Thompson, Vol. 3, pp. 518–19.

185. *Minutes*, PCUS, 1959, p. 69; *BC*, 6.137–6.138.

186. Eric Mount, Jr., and Johanna W. H. Bos, "Scripture on Sexuality: Shifting Authority," *Journal of Presbyterian History* 59, no. 2 (Summer 1981): 224.

187. *BO*, G-2.0300.

188. *BO*, G-2.0400.

189. *BO*, G-2.0500.

190. Cited in "Assessment," p. 3.

191. "Confessional Nature," p. 10 at 29.205 (a).

Conclusion

1. *BC*, 6.175.

BIBLIOGRAPHY

Address of the General Assembly of the Presbyterian Church in the Confederate States of America to All the Churches of Jesus Christ Throughout the Earth, Adopted Unanimously at the Organization of the General Assembly in Augusta, Ga., December, 1861. N.p.: Published by order of the Assembly, n.d.

Armstrong, Maurice W., Lefferts A. Loetscher, and Charles A. Anderson, eds. *The Presbyterian Enterprise: Sources of American Presbyterian History.* Philadelphia: The Westminster Press, 1956.

"The Assessment of Proposed Amendments to *The Book of Confessions.*" Louisville: Office of Theology and Worship, 1997.

Barton, John. *How the Bible Came to Be.* Louisville: Westminster John Knox Press, 1998.

Biblical Authority and Interpretation. A Resource Document Received by the 194th General Assembly (1982) of the United Presbyterian Church in the United States of America. Louisville: Office of the General Assembly, 1992.

Boyd, Lois A., and R. Douglas Brackenridge. *Presbyterian Women in America: Two Centuries of a Quest for Status.* Contributions to the Study of Religion, No. 9. A Publication of the Presbyterian Historical Society. Westport, Conn.: Greenwood Press, 1983.

Buckley, Thomas E., S. J. *"The Great Catastrophe of My Life": Divorce in the Old South.* Unpublished Manuscript, 1998.

Burgess, John. *Why Scripture Matters: Reading the Bible in a Time of Church Conflict.* Louisville: Westminster John Knox Press, 1998.

Carnell, Edward John. *The Case for Orthodox Theology.* Philadelphia: The Westminster Press, 1959.

Carruthers, S. W., ed. *The Confession of Faith of the Assembly of Divines at Westminster, From the Original Manuscript Written by Cornelius Burges in 1646*. N.p.: Presbyterian Church of England, 1946.

———. *Three Centuries of the Westminster Shorter Catechism*, with a Facsimile Reproduction of the Original Manuscript Presented to Parliament, 25th November, 1647. Fredericton, New Brunswick: University of New Brunswick, 1957.

Christie, John W., and Dwight Dumond. *George Bourne and The Book and Slavery Irreconcilable*. Presbyterian Historical Society Series, Vol. IX. Wilmington, Del.: The Historical Society of Delaware, 1969.

"The Confessional Nature of the Church." Commended to the Church for Study by the 198th General Assembly (1986) Presbyterian Church (U.S.A.). Louisville: Theology and Worship Ministry Unit, 1986.

The Confessional Statement of the United Presbyterian Church of North America. Pittsburgh: Board of Christian Education of the United Presbyterian Church of North America, 1951.

The Constitution of the Presbyterian Church (U.S.A.). Part I: *Book of Confessions*. Louisville: Office of the General Assembly, 1991.

The Constitution of the Presbyterian Church (U.S.A.). Part II: *Book of Order*. Louisville: Office of the General Assembly, 1997.

Dabney, Robert L. "Anti-Biblical Theories of Rights." *Presbyterian Quarterly* 2, no. 2 (July 1888): 217–42.

Davison, James E. *The Year of the Bible: A Comprehensive, Congregation-Wide Program of Bible Reading*. Louisville: Bridge Resources, 1996.

"A Declaration of Faith (Presbyterian Church in the United States)." In *The Proposed Book of Confessions with Related Documents*. Approved by the 116th General Assembly and Recommended to the Presbyteries for Their Advice and Consent. Atlanta: Presbyterian Church in the United States, 1976.

Dorrien, Gary. *The Remaking of Evangelical Theology*. Louisville: Westminster John Knox Press, 1998.

Dowey, Edward A., Jr. *A Commentary on the Confession of 1967 and An Introduction to the Book of Confessions*. Philadelphia: The Westminster Press, 1968.

Eberts, Harry W., Jr. *We Believe: A Study of the Book of Confessions for Church Officers*. Philadelphia: Geneva Press, 1987.

Emerson, James G., Jr. *Divorce, the Church, and Remarriage*. Philadelphia: The Westminster Press, 1961.

———."The Remarriage of Divorced Persons in the United Presbyterian Church of the United States of America." Ph.D. diss., Divinity School of the University of Chicago, 1959.

Farmer, James Oscar, Jr. *The Metaphysical Confederacy: James Henley Thornwell and the Synthesis of Southern Values.* Macon, Ga.: Mercer University Press, 1986.

Felder, Cain Hope, ed. *Stony the Road We Trod: African American Biblical Interpretation.* Minneapolis: Fortress Press, 1991.

Froehlich, Karlfried. "'Abinadab's Chariot': The Predicament of Biblical Interpretation." *The Princeton Seminary Bulletin* XVIII (1997): 262–78.

Goldingay, John. *Models for Interpretation of Scripture.* Grand Rapids: Eerdmans, 1995.

Gray, Joan S., and Joyce C. Tucker. *Presbyterian Polity for Church Officers.* Third edition. Louisville: Geneva Press, 1999.

Hall, Douglas John. *Remembered Voices: Reclaiming the Legacy of "Neo-Orthodoxy."* Louisville: Westminster John Knox Press, 1998.

Hogeland, Ronald W. "Charles Hodge, The Association of Gentlemen and Ornamental Womanhood: 1825–1855." *Journal of Presbyterian History* 53, no. 3 (Fall 1975): 239–55.

Johnson, Benton. "From Old to New Agendas: Presbyterians and Social Issues in the Twentieth Century." In *The Confessional Mosaic: Presbyterians and Twentieth-Century Theology.* Edited by Milton J. Coalter, John M. Mulder, and Louis B. Weeks. Louisville: Westminster John Knox Press, 1990.

Kirkpatrick, Clifton, and William Hopper, Jr. *What Unites Presbyterians: Common Ground for Troubled Times.* Louisville: Geneva Press, 1997.

Kraft, Charles H. *Christianity in Culture: A Study in Dynamic Biblical Theologizing in Cross-Cultural Perspective.* Maryknoll, N.Y.: Orbis Books, 1979.

Lewis, C. S. *Reflections on the Psalms.* London: Geoffrey Bles, 1958.

Lightfoot, John. *The Whole Works of the Rev. John Lightfoot, D.D.* Edited by the Rev. John Rogers Pitman, A.M. Vol. XIII, Containing The Journal of the Proceedings of the Assembly of Divines: from January 1, 1643, to December 31, 1644, and Letters to and from Dr. Lightfoot. London: J. F. Dove, St. John's Square, 1824.

March, W. Eugene. "'Biblical Theology,' Authority and the Presbyterians." *Journal of Presbyterian History* 59, no. 2 (Summer 1981): 113–29.

McCarthy, David B. "Walter Wynn Kenyon (1948–)." In *Dictionary of Heresy Trials in American Christianity.* Edited by George H. Shriver. Westport, Conn.: Greenwood Press, 1997.

McKim, Donald K., ed. *Encyclopedia of the Reformed Faith.* Louisville: Westminster John Knox Press, 1992.

———. *Westminster Dictionary of Theological Terms.* Louisville: Westminster John Knox Press, 1996.

Minutes, Presbyterian Church in the United States (PCUS): 1916; 1938; 1946; 1953; 1956; 1959.

Minutes, Presbyterian Church in the United States of America (PCUSA): 1910; 1925; 1926; 1927; 1929; 1930; 1953.

Minutes, United Presbyterian Church in the United States of America (UPCUSA): 1978.

Moorhead, James H. "Redefining Confessionalism: American Presbyterians in the Twentieth Century." In *The Confessional Mosaic: Presbyterians and Twentieth-Century Theology.* Edited by Milton J Coalter, John M. Mulder, and Louis B. Weeks. Louisville: Westminster John Knox Press, 1990.

Mount, Eric, Jr., and Johanna W. H. Bos. "Scripture on Sexuality: Shifting Authority." *Journal of Presbyterian History* 59, no. 2 (Summer 1981): 219–41.

Mulder, John M., and Lee A. Wyatt. "The Predicament of Pluralism: The Study of Theology in Presbyterian Seminaries Since the 1920s." In *The Pluralistic Vision: Presbyterians and Mainstream Protestant Education and Leadership.* Edited by Milton J Coalter, John M. Mulder, and Louis B. Weeks. Louisville: Westminster John Knox Press, 1992.

Musser, Donald W., and Joseph L. Price, eds. *A New Handbook of Christian Theology.* Nashville: Abingdon Press, 1992.

Niebuhr, H. Richard. *Christ and Culture.* New York: Harper & Brothers, 1951.

Noll, Mark A. "The Bible and Slavery." In *Religion and the American Civil War.* Edited by Randall M. Miller, Harry S. Stout, and Charles Reagan Wilson. New York: Oxford University Press, 1998.

Presbyterian Understanding and Use of Holy Scripture and Biblical Authority and Interpretation. Position Statement adopted by the

123rd General Assembly (1983) of the Presbyterian Church in the United States. Louisville: Office of the General Assembly, 1992.

Quick, Charles E. "Origins of the Auburn Affirmation." *Journal of Presbyterian History* 53, no. 2 (Summer 1955): 120–42.

———. "A Statistical Analysis of the Signers of the Auburn Affirmation." *Journal of Presbyterian History* 43, no. 3 (Fall 1965): 182–96.

"Report of the Ad Interim Committee on a Biblical Study of the Position of Women in the Church." General Assembly *Minutes* (PCUS), 1956: 138–42.

"Report of the Committee on Pluralism in the Church to the 190th General Assembly (1978) of the United Presbyterian Church in the United States of America." *Minutes*, 1978, Part I.

Report of the Special Committee on a Brief Contemporary Statement of Faith to the 177th General Assembly, the United Presbyterian Church in the United States of America, May 1965. Philadelphia: Office of the General Assembly, 1965.

Robinson, John. *The Testimony and Practice of the Presbyterian Church in Reference to American Slavery with an Appendix: Containing the Position of the General Assembly (New School), Free Presbyterian Church, Reformed Presbyterian, Associate, Associate Reformed, Baptist, Protestant Episcopal, and Methodist Episcopal Churches.* Cincinnati: John D. Thorpe, 1852.

Rogers, Jack B. "Biblical Authority and Confessional Change." *Journal of Presbyterian History* 59, no. 2 (Summer 1981): 131–56.

Rogers, Jack. *Claiming the Center: Churches and Conflicting Worldviews.* Louisville: Westminster John Knox Press, 1995.

Rogers, Jack. "The Kenyon Case." In *Women and Men in Ministry.* Edited by Roberta Hestenes. Pasadena: Fuller Theological Seminary, 1985.

Rogers, Jack. *Presbyterian Creeds: A Guide to the Book of Confessions.* Revised edition. Louisville: Westminster John Knox Press, 1991.

Rogers, Jack Bartlett. *Scripture in the Westminster Confession: A Problem of Historical Interpretation for American Presbyterianism.* Grand Rapids: Eerdmans, 1967.

Rogers, Jack B., and Donald K. McKim. *The Authority and Interpretation of the Bible: An Historical Approach.* San Francisco: Harper & Row, 1979.

Rohls, Jan. *Reformed Confessions: Theology from Zurich to Barmen.*

Translated by John Hoffmeyer. Introduction by Jack L. Stotts. Columbia Series in Reformed Theology. Louisville: Westminster John Knox Press, 1998.

Russell, Letty M., ed. *Feminist Interpretation of the Bible*. Philadelphia: The Westminster Press, 1985.

Sanders, Marthame E., III. "'A Fellowship of Concern,' and the Declining Doctrine of the Spirituality of the Church in the Presbyterian Church in the United States." *Journal of Presbyterian History* 75, no. 3 (Fall 1997): 179–95.

Scott, Karen (Bear) Ride. "Expanding the Horizons of Ministry: Women of the Cloth in the Presbyterian Church, U.S.A." D. Min. diss. project, San Francisco Theological Seminary, 1990.

Scouller, James Brown. *A History of the United Presbyterian Church of North America*. In *A History of The Methodist Church, South; The United Presbyterian Church; The Cumberland Presbyterian Church and The Presbyterian Church, South in the United States*. Edited by Gross Alexander, James B. Scouller, R. V. Foster, and T. C. Johnson. The American Church History Series, Vol. XI. New York: The Christian Literature Co., 1894.

Smylie, James H. *A Brief History of the Presbyterians*. Louisville: Geneva Press, 1996.

Stowe, Harriet Beecher. *Uncle Tom's Cabin or Life Among the Lowly*. Boston: Houghton, Mifflin & Co., 1892. Original edition, 1851.

Tharp, Roland G., and Ronald Gallimore. "Basketball's John Wooden: What a Coach Can Teach a Teacher." *Psychology Today* 9, no. 8 (January 1976): 75–78.

Thompson, Ernest Trice. *Presbyterians in the South, Volume One: 1607–1861*. Richmond: John Knox Press, 1963.

———. *Presbyterians in the South, Volume Two: 1861–1890*. Richmond: John Knox Press, 1973.

———. *Presbyterians in the South, Volume Three: 1890–1972*. Richmond: John Knox Press, 1973.

Thompson, Robert Ellis. *A History of the Presbyterian Churches in the United States*. The American Church History Series, Vol. VI. New York: The Christian Literature Co., 1895.

Trinterud, Leonard J. *The Forming of An American Tradition: A Reexamination of Colonial Presbyterianism*. Philadelphia: The Westminster Press, 1949.

White, Ronald C., Jr. "Social Witness and Evangelism." In *How Shall We Witness? Faithful Evangelism in a Reformed Tradition*. Edited by Milton J Coalter and Virgil Cruz. Louisville: Westminster John Knox Press, 1995.